D1825510

DIARY

OF A

MAD BAND DIRECTOR

D*I*ARY

OF A
MAD BAND DIRECTOR

T. D. HOLLINS

To order additional copies of this book, contact:
Xlibris
1-888-795-4274
www.Xlibris.com
Orders@Xlibris.com
780682

CONTENTS

Part C : Sound Living

Preface

This might be my last year—my fifteenth year—not because I let it beat me but because I have finally won. I've found the happiness that I've been searching for all my life. Ironically, I found it in a place that has nothing to do with music. You see, happiness is the single "life essential" that we all long for. We feel happiness when we perform. We feel happiness when we have successful lessons that indicate student learning. We feel happiness when our peers, our colleagues, and our communities love what we have provided. This happiness is what I now refer to as *sound living*. It has been a journey to finally "live sound." It is difficult for us music educators to find that true happiness because we often end up having a conflicting relationship with our passion.

Any musician can tell you that it is passion that motivates us to practice, perform, compose, and teach. That same passion can also lead us to neglect our family, become arrogant, isolate ourselves, become socially awkward, and feel internally miserable. Living our passion sometimes comes at a cost. It can come in the form of low pay, long hours, jealous coworkers, and narcissistic administrators if you work for an organization. If you couple that with a nonunderstanding support system at home, it can lead to a mental and physical breakdown if you are not careful.

But our passion makes us get up every day and do it again. Passion can be like a drug addiction or an abusive relationship. We need to feel needed. We need that love. We need learning to take place. We need that feeling that we get from positive comments and warm rounds of applause. We get a rush off the world loving what we give. Madness lives in that space between us sharing the results of our passion with the world, at the expense of being underpaid, underappreciated, overworked, and overwhelmed.

This might be my last year, but I have so much that I need to share so that the future educators, organizational leaders, administrators, support systems, and curious minds can understand the business behind the music of a passionate educator during a journey to find true happiness.

I've been a musician since I was eight years old. Music was my life. But now music is only a vehicle that I use to help others find their happiness. My experience in teaching, coaching, and mentoring has driven me to write about my story and some tips based on my experiences. It's a story of passion—a passion that almost drove me *mad*. This is my diary—the diary of a mad band director.

This book is designed to

1. assist all newly hired band directors during the transitional point between the "contract signing" and the first performance,
2. serve as a guide for returning band directors for consistency in operational procedures and preparation for upcoming years, and
3. provide transparent basic operational procedures for supervisors as a means of guiding new hires during this transition.

Part A

LET THE MADNESS BEGIN: SEEDS, SORROWS, AND SUCCESSES

Chapter 1

THE SEEDS OF MY PASSION (1985)

In 1985, I started taking piano lessons from an old lady at the church named Ms. Ionia. I'm not sure if the lessons were free or my mom scraped up some funds to make them happen. All I knew was that I wanted to play, and my mom somehow made it possible. During the first year, I was pretty consistent with practicing and attending lessons. Mom even bought me a Casio keyboard to practice my scales and assignments out of the *My First Lessons* piano book. I really enjoyed the "Snake Charmer," probably because I heard it on an episode of *Tom and Jerry*. It is interesting that you get motivated mostly by being able to play something that you've unconsciously experienced before.

The next year, I played football. I was actually pretty good. I was one of the smallest players, so I focused on being the fastest and hardest-hitting player on the team. As the year progressed, my football schedule and my piano lessons conflicted. I would attend piano classes when I didn't have football practice, but I didn't progress much because my focus was more on sports. This would probably be the first time that I realized that you become what you did the most. I practiced football every day, so I improved every day.

At the end of the season, we ended up losing the championship game to my cousin's team, marking the end of my football career. Then Ms. Ionia ended up abruptly passing away. Needless to say, I pretty much stopped playing piano after she died. I requested to play some songs for the church's youth choir that I learned by rote. I practiced all week, but I just could not grasp some of the chord changes and the finger placement. I guess I shouldn't have skipped those lessons.

Sunday came quickly. I was determined to do my best, but I froze in the middle of the first stanza. The choir continued singing a cappella (without the piano) until the official organist picked up to the accompaniment. I sat there, staring at the piano keys for about thirty seconds, then embarrassingly walked out in the middle of the performance. I cried my eyes out. My uncle Trig came to offer his support and encouragement. Though he made me feel better, I had already made my mind up that I would never play piano again. My uncle Trig gave me his trumpet soon afterward. I often wondered if he knew piano wasn't the right instrument for me or if he just wanted to cheer me up by just giving me a gift. Either way, I was scarred because of the ivory experience.

When boredom set in, I would pick up the trumpet and attempt to push air through but could never produce a sound. At times, I would hum songs through it because I didn't realize that you had to buzz in order to produce a sound. That was the closest I could get to creating music. One day, Uncle Trig explained that you had to create vibration in the mouthpiece in order to get a real tone out of the instrument. After my uncle provided that "magical knowledge" about buzzing, I would just experiment during my moments of boredom.

Within the next year or two, Uncle Larry created a high school alumni band and allowed me to participate. I had no experience reading trumpet music at the time, but somehow I was able to figure out a few songs to teach the band by rote. My first arrangement at age eleven was "Now That We've Found Love" by Heavy D. I was extremely proud that a group of adults were playing a song that I introduced. This encouragement was what I needed to continue playing and learning. I ended up joining middle-school band that next year.

It's interesting how you can pick up things by being bored. I guess having access to positive things during times of boredom can work out for you in the future. I found the opposite to be true as well. I now realize that these experiences laid the foundation for my musical future. I owe it all to my mom, Ms. Ionia, and my uncle Trig. They planted the musical seeds.

Chapter 2

THE ROOT OF MY PASSION (1989)

When I began middle school in 1989, I had some experience with a band. Well, at least I knew how to buzz. I could read a little bass and treble clef because of my piano experience. Who knew that those piano lessons with Ms. Ionia would pay off? Who knew? I had some great middle-school teachers, but for some reason, they did not stick. Each year of middle school, I had a different teacher. I don't remember much about middle-school band besides one of my classmates placing a snare-drum case in the corner of the band room and actually used the pay phone to do a bomb threat because he didn't want to come to school. That was an action-packed day. The most exciting part was watching the bomb squad carry a drum case out as if it were an explosive device. Nevertheless, I never saw the kid again. During, my eighth grade, I ended up switching to baritone and enjoyed it. This instrument was different. It was too big for the bus, but it has a smooth sound. It was odd like me. I figured that I could use this oddness to be different.

During the late eighties, there were a lot of drugs and violence in the community. The crack epidemic hit the streets hard, even in the rural south. To combat this, one of the community leaders developed a group called the NIKE POSSEE. I can't even remember what the acronym meant, but the group was designed to give the teenagers some activities to do. Mostly, the group was popular for hosting talent shows. Back in these times, hip-hop was thriving. We grew up either break-dancing or having freestyle rap ciphers in the front yard, at school recess, or anywhere else we congregated. My friends and I put together a dance group we called BBN (Black by Nature). Since we were six little middle-school guys, we decided to make up a routine to ABC's "Playground." We put in work and actually won $500 at the talent show

It became very difficult to stay positive in an environment so negative. One day, while practicing, a guy whom we didn't like came walking down the street. We decided to jump on him. I didn't know who threw the first punch, but he ended up on the ground in a fetal position while ten little middle schoolers' feet kicked him in the ribs, head, and face. On that day, the dance group changed to something else. All of us ended up getting into different things. Some took the streets. Some ended up getting arrested and quitting school. My attitude had even changed. I got in a few fights in the neighborhood and became disrespectful to some adults. My grandfather passed away, and dividing his assets created a family feud. I even stopped playing my horn on a regular basis. It seemed like everything was falling apart. I became angry and lost.

After a few exchanges with my mother—some verbal, some physical—she put me in my place. Middle school was a very emotional time. I went from being an inspired young musician to an angry young person. This experience was useful later when I started teaching. When a kid acts out of character, there is always a reason. We have to be careful not to give up on those kids. They just need someone to care. My mother cared enough to remove me from that environment before it was too late.

Chapter 3

GROWING PAINS (1992)

About a year after my grandfather passed away, my mom got tired of commuting thirty minutes to the neighboring county for work. That thirty-mile move seemed as if it were states away. I had no friends. I left the family and friends whom I had grown up with since the age of three. This was another very emotional time for me, but remember, I had a "badass" persona that I took with me to the new school. I was convinced that since I looked like O-Dog from *Menace to Society,* no one would bother me. Boy would I be wrong.

One good thing that came out of the move was that I would have the opportunity to join an award-winning high school band program. Unfortunately, I showed up late for band camp. If you have experience with corps-style marching bands, you know that if you are late and there are no holes, you have to wait until the next year. All the trumpet and baritone spots were full, but the band director asked if I mind playing cymbals. I agreed. So in my first year of band, I played cymbals in the marching band, and I played trumpet in class. Sometimes you have to take the opportunity that is given to you and prove that you deserve better.

I would learn very quickly that the guys in this program were serious about music. They had solid fundamentals, and I realized that I was missing a whole lot (probably because of the inconsistency in band directors). I remember one day as we were preparing for district band auditions, a guy told me, "You are definitely not going to make it sounding like that." That crushed and motivated me simultaneously. I didn't make it, but I learned that I had to do more if I wanted to be successful.

During the first day of school, I felt as if I were in the busy New York streets at rush hour. The halls were filled with students. I remember an upper classmen bumped me and said, "What you wanna do?" That translated into "I'll beat your little ass." This wouldn't be the only situation like this. I quickly began to hate this place.

Despite all the crazy situations in high school, trying to avoid getting jumped on by all the athletic teams and the high school dope boys, getting police escorts home, being misunderstood and misinterpreted by those who didn't personally know me, I managed to become a great musician during that time. Music became my best friend. I started out with no friends. I had a couple of cousins at the school, but they were already accepted by their peers. I was the only kid in the county with dreadlocks. I wore my brother's hand-me-downs, but they were better than a lot of what the other kids were wearing. I had the latest Karl Kani and Cross Colour outfits. Those were popular brands at the time. Also, I was getting a little attention because I was the new guy, and the local guys were not feeling that at all. This caused me to isolate myself. So I turned to music.

The summer after my freshman year, I decided that I would practice every day until I got better. I didn't have many resources, but my uncle left a rhythm book in the trumpet that he left at my house when I was ten years old. I never paid that book any mind until that summer. I played the entire book that summer on one note. I figured that if I could correctly play every rhythm and not have to simultaneously think about the fingerings of notes, I would be halfway there. Oddly, it must have worked. The next year, I switched to baritone and made first chair at All District and All County and fourth chair at South Carolina all-state auditions. From cymbals to fourth chair in the state of South Carolina! Ironically, after I got good on my instrument, I instantly became cool. I actually had four friends. I was on my way!

The harassment at school did not stop as I matriculated. It got to the point that I was carrying a weapon to school every day. I learned how to stay out of places and situations that could get me in trouble. I actually avoided suspension and fighting until my senior year. The band room became a refuge for me. I felt safe there. It was a place where I was able to express myself musically. It was as if every time something happened, I unconsciously turned to music. There are so many kids that find comfort in the band room. Yes, music is important, but sometimes their loyalty to the program is deeper than actually playing.

High school was a crazy experience filled with social challenges, but I have always embraced a challenge. I didn't have the natural talent, but when faced with doubters, I took some hard looks in the mirror. I didn't have the resources, but I was resourceful. I knew that anything was possible with work. These were all the pains of growing up and overcoming obstacles, though I socially lacked confidence. I ended up finding my confidence in my talent. It became my voice, my vehicle for expression, and my ticket to college.

Chapter 4

ROOTS GROWING DOWN? (1996)

In 1996, I graduated and decided to attend college in Atlanta, Georgia. Atlanta was a huge city to a country boy like myself. The buildings were taller than two stories. The mall had two levels and an ice-skating rink. They had real traffic like a real rush hour. The best part about it all was that all my high school friends came to school here too. Interestingly, we ended up being some of the best players in the program.

A band camp was a duplication of military basic training. We had 5:00 a.m. calisthenics, thirty-minute meals, and maybe four hours of sleep per night. Outside of the physical demands, being a freshman didn't make it any easier. During those days, they referred to freshmen as *crabs* or *white shirts*. We hadn't earned the right to wear the school colors until we passed certain criteria by the end of band camp. Even at that point, we wouldn't be considered full band members until we made it through homecoming. We were ridiculed, we were forced to eat last, and we sang silly songs. Some of the sections actually required some physical rituals and rites of passages in order to be accepted as a full member. Personally, I tried to stay out of the way of the veteran members. I remained focus on playing my horn. That saved me from a lot of the harsh punishment.

Despite the freshman initiation stuff, I actually enjoyed the semester as a band member. The director Mr. Love was a very skilled motivator. He brought the energy out of us. The crowd could feel our passion for performing, so we received many standing ovations that year. Musically, our program wasn't very strong, but the showmanship aspect was so undeniably compelling, you wouldn't notice unless you had a musician's ear. I learned a lot about what crowds generally enjoy during this experience. Later, I would only use that "secret weapon" after I drew them into our musical performances.

During our first class meeting at the beginning of the semester, the dean of the college informed the group that the university would no longer be offering music as a major. I couldn't believe it. At that point, I knew that I would be leaving. I began looking at other music colleges and their curriculum. I enrolled in classes that I thought matched up, passed them, and transferred to a college in North Carolina to pursue my dreams of being a band director. Sometimes it is important for roots to grow down so they can explore the soil and maximize their water uptake. Right at the point where I thought I was about to sprout as a musician, I was knocked down. I found out that growth happens when you are uncomfortable. You just have to fight your way through obstacles. I fought through it, planned my move, and transferred to another college.

Chapter 5

ROOTS SPREADING (1997)

At my new college in North Carolina, I experienced true musical aesthetics. The feeling that I received while playing in that group—coupled with the focus on balance and blend, true tone quality, and dynamic contrast—was reminiscent of my high school days. I gained all my emotional connection to music from my experience in those rehearsals. Ironically, this was the place where I found my wife and true love. My love affair with the band program paralleled the love for my future wife.

Unfortunately, every relationship has its ups and downs. My girlfriend left school for a year and a half because of financial troubles, and our awesome band director Mr. Runner was released from his position. Mr. Runner was great; however, there was a side to him that was very tough and could be seen as combative to upper-level administration. I recall playing at commencement, and the dignitaries and administrative team were in place and ready to proceed with the ceremony. The head marshal signaled for the band director to stop playing. The vice chancellor signaled for the band director to stop playing. Then the president signaled for the band director to cut off the band. The director continued conducting, and instead of cueing the band with his left hand, he actually acknowledged the administration's request with a middle finger as he continued with the "Crown Imperial" to the end. Interactions such as this ultimately led to his dismissal. I learned so much from my first year in North Carolina. Balance and blend are just as important as the relationship you build at the school.

Dr. Chevy was hired. It wasn't an easy transition because of the firing of Mr. Runner. During the summer, the veteran band members called for a boycott. It was unsuccessful because most people who were returning were on band scholarship. Plus, we loved the band, not just the band director. After we got through the fights about tradition, we learned to respect and love our new band director. He was a true businessman. He was able to garner support from the administration. We received increases in scholarship funding, purchased new instruments, purchased new uniforms, and even got a staff. Doc demanded that we exemplify leadership and discipline twenty-four hours a day. In 1999, the band staff expanded. When associate band director Mr. Flier came in, we went to an entirely new level.

Our first experience with Mr. Flier was helping him move in his house. Though we were helping, he questioned all our work ethic. He wasn't scared to approach us aggressively and say exactly what was on his mind. He had nothing to prove. He had written our school's theme song twenty years prior to his return to our school, so the respect level was already in place. That night helping him move, we learned so much about musical composition, life, and of course, women. By the time we finished moving, it almost felt as if we needed to compensate him for allowing us to be in his presence. It was a very intense situation.

Rehearsals were just as intense. Nothing was ever perfect to Mr. Flier. During camp, the band was having trouble memorizing a march. To show that we were simply not taking the required work seriously, he came in and played every section's part by memory! We loved and hated him. He was a stickler for perfect logistics and time. He called the band a quasi-military unit. We would conduct ourselves as such, or we would be dismissed. That was the remainder of my band experience there.

Classes went great. I joined a fraternity. I moved off campus. I was achieving academically, and I was having the time of my life. I partied very hard. Again, I stopped practicing.

Socially, I made some horrible decisions that led to me having to do some community service and being placed on probation. I couldn't leave the state of North Carolina for two years, and to top it all off, my girlfriend and future wife became pregnant. So now I'm faced with trying to find a job to take care of my future family while living out my last few months of college.

After receiving my refund check, one day, I sent a message to the band that I was going to have a cook out at my apartment. My refund check hit. Of course, everyone showed up, and we had a great time. Around two hours into the party, we heard a knock on the door, and it was Mr. Flier. Everyone tried not to make it a big deal and continued with the festivities. He came directly to me and said, "Son, do you want to graduate?"

"Yes, sir," I replied.

He continued, "Have you been practicing for your recital?"

"Not like I should, sir," I replied.

He said, "If you want to graduate, you need to be in my fucking office ready to play on Monday. I have been charged with getting you through this damn recital, and I'm not going to look bad!"

"Yes, sir. I'll be there," I replied.

His demeanor then changed, and he said, "Now give me one of those beers!"

I loved him for that. He knew how to break us down with tough love and then build us up enough that we were encouraged enough to produce. He proceeded to give me his portfolio that night just to read all the things that he had accomplished. It was quite impressive to say the least. He was basically a prodigy. I learned that it is important that we do great things so we can inspire the next generation of thinkers and doers. I proceeded to practice and do great at my recital.

One week later, as I was walking through the fine arts building with my classmates, the department's administrative assistant yelled,

"It's someone on the phone from Greensboro looking for a band director!"

The group of graduating music majors that I was walking with were uninterested, but I knew I would be having a baby in three months. So I took the call, got interviewed, graduated, and moved to Greensboro. The next four years would be the beginning of my journey as a music educator.

Chapter 6

SOWING SEEDS (2001)

I couldn't believe it! I got offered my first band and a salary of $35,000 per year. I thought I was rich back then, just because my check went from having two zeroes to three zeroes. And to think if I stay in the job twenty more years, I could make a whopping $50,000 a year! Pretty sad if you think about it. We have been taught that we don't get into teaching simply for a paycheck. We get into it because we are passionate about student success. At this point, I was as passionate as I could get and as broke as I could get too.

This school system in the Greensboro area was a great place to work. Each student in the entire county was supplied with their own personal laptop to use at school and at home. We had a budget that was suitable for a high-school band program, and I didn't have any scheduling issues. I had a successful feeder middle-school program that was so large that they had two band directors. The community was hungry for a change in band culture. They wanted to see more exciting shows and a more interactive stand presence to support the strong athletic teams. The students were eager for a change as well. They wanted to incorporate more top forty selections in their repertoire. They wanted to continue to grow musically, but they also wanted to feel "cool."

I brought my leadership team in first (section leaders and drum majors). We did team-building activities. We discussed the direction of the program and the goals for the season. This time enabled us to get on one accord and have the stills to transfer our training to the other bandmates when they arrived.

When the band arrived, the leadership team sprang into action. With the help of guest clinicians, we were able to push them mentally, physically, and most importantly, musically. They had the pride and determination to be the best band in the region.

In October of that year, we felt that our show was ready to showcase at a competition, so I returned to my alma mater to participate in theirs. There were some great programs led by many of my colleagues, peers, and mentors. We were so nervous during the awards. When they called our name to receive the participant plaque, the students cheered so loud, you would have thought that we won the competition. After the participation plaques were distributed, we eagerly waited for them to announce our school's name. They called the drum major awards. Nothing. They called the majorette awards. Nothing. They called the flag awards. Nothing. They called the dancer awards. We received fourth place in dance. They called the marching awards. Nothing. They called the music awards. Nothing. They called the overall band awards. Nothing. I looked at the band, and they held their heads low in disappointment.

When we returned to school, I discussed the judges' comments with the students. Most of the comments were valid. I didn't discuss the ones that I disagreed with. Though it wasn't a perfectly judged competition, I thought that it gave us a measuring stick for success and provided enough assessment to get back to work. On that day, we made the decision to never leave another competition disappointed. So we went to work.

The next week, we attended another competition and received first place in our class. This tradition of excellence continued into the next year when we won grand champion at every competition we participated in. The entire community rallied behind us. We became the face of the school receiving national recognition for winning competitions on the local, regional, and national levels. We were recognized by the local news outlets, newspapers, magazines, and even the state board of education. It was a great time for the program. Then fear set in.

I had worked all my life to become a great musician and band director, and in my second year of teaching, my band program was being labeled "one of the best bands in the country." It was a happy time but a lonely time as well. What would we do next? I challenged the students by attending state concert and jazz band festivals. We got superiors at both. I challenged them individually through assessing them in class and by attending district and county band clinics. At least 25 percent of our students made the bands. Ironically, everything that I challenged them to do, they met with enthusiasm. Most directors would be happy with this setup, but for a twenty-four-year-old, it was a lot to handle.

I felt that I had accomplished things that took my mentors ten years to accomplish. I didn't have an answer for "What's next?" Maybe it was because I was young, or maybe it was the network of people that I was associated with. No one could share the story with me. In retrospect, I realized that I should have been more active with professional-development opportunities so that I could see that there was more to accomplish. Needless to say that when I hit that level of success so early, I started seeking other opportunities. I wanted to begin my quest to become a collegiate band director.

Did I have challenges? Oh yeah! I made many, many mistakes. I recall on the way back from a band competition, our buses got separated. I was on the first bus, and we were far ahead of the rest of the band so we arrived at school first. (Remember, cell phones were at the beginning stages of popularity at that time.) I got a call in the office as we were waiting for the rest of the band. On the other line was one of my colleagues who was traveling the same route. He indicated to me that he saw my buses on the side of the road, and he thought they had been in an accident. I immediately panicked because I had all the medical forms on my bus.

About thirty minutes passed, and one of the band parents came to update me. The bus was hit by a car, but no one was hurt. We had one kid that claimed he was having a back pain, so the ambulance checked him out. As the third bus approached the accident, the students noticed that one of our band members was in the ambulance, and the students went hysterical. Some of them were asthmatics and began hyperventilating. Others were crying and becoming sick, so the medics decided that they would take the entire band to the hospitals around Greensboro. Without having any recorded list, they proceeded to split the band up around six different hospitals in the Greensboro area. And then the calls began.

Our return time was scheduled for 5:00 p.m., but two-thirds of the band (approximately eighty students) were at the hospitals and unaccounted for. We spent the next five hours trying to figure out where the students were so we could get the parents to pick them up. I got home at 1:00 a.m. after leaving at 9:00 a.m. the previous day. I learned from that moment to always have a copy of the medical forms on all books, keep a very detailed bus list, and never allow our buses to separate.

I also experienced the following:

1. The band boosters told the bus driver that the band was ready to depart, so they left without me.
2. The band parents felt that they could control the band operations.
3. Students got caught with drugs or alcohol on trips.
4. Students got caught making out in the bathrooms.
5. There were hotel complaints.
6. Students were abused at home.
7. There were multiple student deaths.

I wore the hat of a teacher, musician, fundraiser, conductor, custodian, coordinator, administrator, repairman, babysitter, publicist, designer, salesman, manager, parent, counselor, mentor, teacher, coach, accountant, advocate, and role model.

I just couldn't drop the band off and go home. I didn't just have my personal problems anymore. I had a responsibility that extended far beyond the dismissal bell. I was a band director—an award-winning band director. That meant that I belonged to the students, school, community, and entire network of music educators. This is what I signed up for, and now I needed to figure out the next move.

When you succeed, opportunities begin to knock. During my final two years at the high school, I was offered an opportunity to be interviewed in multiple high schools and one college. I wasn't selected for any of them. This was humbling, but I was still winning, so I continued to work as usual. One day, my principal called me in to congratulate me on receiving an award. The conversation seemed a little awkward because he kept pointing out that the band program seemed bigger than the school. I sensed jealousy. My principal was new, and this was his first year in a principal position. Sometimes insecure supervisors do not see that if the entities at their school succeed, we *all* succeed. We actually make them look good. He continued the conversation by saying that when I decided to leave the school, I could take the band plaque in his office with me. I politely said "thank you" and waited for the reason for this meeting. After leaving with a sense of confusion, I realized that I should probably make sure I kept my nose clean because I couldn't determine if the head administrator was for or against having a successful band program and a popular band director.

Not long after, I called my old college band director Dr. Chevy to seek some advice, but before I could get to the purpose of the call, he scolded me for not telling him that I had applied for a position near the college. I Securing that position could have potentially set up a great feeder situation for the college program. He informed me that the local school principal called him and said they didn't hire me because I received a bad reference from my current employer. My punk ass principal! I realized at that point that my principal did not want me to leave. He actually went to the length of lying on my reference! I could not believe it. This was a very good lesson. Make sure your references are genuine colleagues. Be sure that the people you list are secure enough in their own lives that they won't be envious by seeing your career development. Everybody isn't for you. At that point, I realized that I needed to move on with my career.

After a discussion with my wife, I looked at the map and decided on three locations where I could work and peruse my master's degree: Columbia, South Carolina; Washington DC; Charlotte, North Carolina; or Atlanta, Georgia. After weighing our options, we decided on Atlanta. At that time, the school system there had a program that would pay 100 percent tuition remission for teachers pursuing their master's degree. I attended a job fair and was offered a job. I packed up my family and left my award-winning program. I knew they would be okay because I planted similar developmental seeds that were planted in me growing up. I was simply sowing. I wanted more. Well, I felt a passion for more. That summer, we became pregnant with my second child. My family needed more; we were back to Atlanta.

Chapter 7

SPROUTING (2005)

I was so excited to be moving back to Atlanta as a working adult. I had friends there. It was a city for young people. It had a thriving nightlife, and the opportunities for growth experiences were prevalent. I decided to teach middle school for two reasons: to force myself to get more acquainted with my secondary instruments and to free up my nights and weekends for graduate school.

School started out great. My classes were small, and my schedule was free for two periods in one day. I used those two periods to write papers and study for my night classes. For my sixth grade class, I just figured that I would just stay a few pages ahead of my classes in the book so I could always appear to be the hero. I had my lessons planned out all the way to the holiday break in December. Middle school was going to be a piece of cake in my mind.

After about a week of interactive lessons, I figured that I could loosen up on the discipline in my classes. Huge mistake. Kids needed consistency. They needed clear expectations, and they needed to see how they are developing. I figured that I could give my class a "break" for doing well and learning their lessons in one week. That next week, I immediately realized that I had lost my class, and it would take a long time to get them back. I had broken my own regiment that was working, simply because I was bored with the monotony. My classes began to be more motivated by getting a day off than actually learning to become better musicians. It took half of the year to get back on track.

I had many other issues at this school as well. English was the second language for 70 percent of my class. In fact, I had some classes that students could only say hello and goodbye. I learned to use my bilingual kids to help translate the lessons for me.

Fifty percent of my class was reading at below grade level. I had one written assignment where the students had to write the name of the class at the type of the page, and they wrote "BAN CLASS." I learned that reading was a conversation with writing. Most kids that couldn't read had trouble writing as well.

Thirty percent of my class were labeled "special education." Ironically, most of them were the ESL (English as a second language) kids. I guess they didn't know how else to label their inability to communicate and learn subjects because of the language barrier. That made no sense to me.

Twenty-five percent of my class had an IEP (individual education plan) that included behavior modifications. These kids were mostly emotionally disturbed because of a traumatic experience or other disability. I had kids pulling out other student's hair. I'd seen a teacher slap a student and vice versa. I broke up many fights in the hallways and the cafeteria. One day, in a faculty meeting, the administration told us that "cursing" was not a punishable offense. In other words, if a student cursed at us, we could not send them to the office or write them up. I also remember one week, the entire seventh-grade hallway of teachers called out of work, which forced all the elective teachers to cover their classes during our planning periods. This school was failing, but I signed up for it, so I had to finish the job.

You see, in order to receive tuition remission for graduate school, I had to teach at a Title I school. At this school, 90 percent of the students received free or reduced lunch. Some of the kids lived in hotels and only ate meals at school. My heart went out to my students. I really enjoyed listening to their stories and mentoring them through their problems. Hell, I had received reduced lunch growing up. I was raised by a single parent too. So I could identify with them on some levels. What I didn't identify with was not having a supportive parent. So to witness parents telling the administrators to just "take him to jail because I can't do anything with him" broke my heart. I knew that I couldn't stay here. The state came in to provide support to the teachers and administrators, and the school closed down three years later. I decided to do my two years and get out as soon as possible.

By December, it was performance time. We did our "Jingle Bells" with a hip-hop mix, and the student body, parents, and teachers were pleased. We sparked enough interest in the program that it jumped from 50 people to 110 the next year.

During the summer of year two, I was asked to be the assistant band director at the same local college in Atlanta where I spent my first year in undergraduate school. I was so excited for the opportunity! I explained to the collegiate band director that my schedule was pretty hectic and that my time would be limited because of my middle school and grad school obligations. The director seemed to be okay with that. He was a bit of a micromanager anyway, so I decided to do only what was required and nothing more. Sometimes as an assistant, you have to do just that—*assist*. You may not like your supervisor's approach to things, but keep an open communication. If you see something, you can ask if the supervisor minds if you step in to address the problem. Just be careful how much you impose your ideologies onto someone else's band. It can cause a strain in your relationship.

This collegiate band program in Atlanta had diminished so much because of the changeover in directors. The students had lost their passion and drive for the program. They were unsure about the direction of the band. They were imploding.

After the holiday break, I think the band director had become totally frustrated. He stopped communicating with me and did not show back up to work. After about two weeks, the administration called me in and offered to compensate me for working with the college band for the semester, and I, of course, took the offer, not just for the compensation but for the students. I cared about the reputation of the university, and I cared about healing a broken program.

That semester, I finished graduate school while working middle school during the day and college in the evenings. I sacrificed a lot of time away from my family because I cared. I guess that passion was kicking back in. June came around, and I received a call to the president's office. The university president told me to bring my transcripts from graduate school. I told her that I would be finishing my last class in July and graduating in August. At the end of that meeting, she offered me the job as a head director.

At age twenty-seven, I was a collegiate band director. It was my time to shine. I always knew that if I just worked hard, good things would come. I wasn't focused on money. I just believed that I needed to get that degree and position myself for the next move. I knew that I had to be qualified if the opportunity ever knocked. So I positioned myself to win. I let my passion guide me that next year as the head collegiate band director. We had a great year. I was finally living my passion. It heavily burned within my soul to succeed, and . . . I totally burned out.

Sometimes when you move too fast, you begin to believe that the band is actually yours, but it is not. It is the university's band. It belongs to the people that come after you. You are simply in charge of it for however long that you have the opportunity to serve. It is your job to take care of it so the future students and directors will have their shot. I had great intentions that were driven by my passion for the students. Sometimes *your* passion and plans do not perfectly align with the person in charge. That nonalignment led to my final letter to the band. My contract wasn't renewed, and I had been displaced.

Chapter 8

UPROOTED: THE FINAL LETTER TO THE BAND (2006)

Dear Band Staff and Students Past and Present,

I remember sitting on the fifty-yard line in 1992 at a college football game in Columbia, South Carolina. That was the day that I decided that music would be a part of my life.

In 1996, a very well-dressed gentleman came to my small-town high school and gave me the impression that his college band was larger than life. I had never seen the band or heard of the institution, but his presentation was so convincing that I believed that there was a great opportunity there in Atlanta, only to arrive in August with the disturbing information that the administration decided to suspend the music education major. Clue no. 1 that there was no sense of importance for music at the institution.

So I decided to further my studies in North Carolina—the best musical decision that I've made. However, in 1997, the school was a disaster. The program was imploding from a series of internal problems. In 1998, a new director took over, marking the rebuilding of the program. During my entire musical experience in North Carolina, the band was in transition, but it was a consistent and strategic plan for growth. I learned my entire strategy for building a program and creating musicians from mediocre players through my experience as a section leader in that band. During this time, I studied with many great professors and staff members. I remember when we got new uniforms and instruments. My frat brothers along with other members stayed that summer and numbered every stand and instrument. I was on work study, and I remember putting every director's and potential student's name in a database. I also remember transitioning the music library from manuscript to Finale Notation Software. We were manually inputting scores on Finale. Let me back up. I met my wife at an orientation in July 1997, not knowing that we would be married later. She was the first person whom I met. We didn't even know that we were both going to be in a band until we saw each other again at band camp. We didn't talk much in the cafeteria where we met. But I digress.

In 2001, I was blessed with a son, which was one of my motivations to get my *bleep* out of school and get a job. At the age of twenty-two, I was offered a position in Greensboro, North Carolina. I remember being in the cafeteria, and the ladies would say, "You can't jump in line, honey!" They mistook me for one of the students at least once a week for the first nine weeks. My first senior class consisted of some great leaders who attended colleges all over the United States. My students not only attended college but also were leaders in the band programs. Many have already graduated. While at high school, we won a national high school marching band competition and continued to win everything since. In addition, the band had received only superior and excellent ratings at concert and jazz band festivals, all before the age of twenty-five. I left Greensboro in 2005 to pursue my masters. I relocated to Atlanta.

I taught middle school for two years, but who would have figured that I would end up in Atlanta at the very place where I started my collegiate musical experience? Who would have thought that life would lead me back to the very place where I stamped those school initials in my brain and on my heart? To the band program in which nothing was given, you had to earn everything that you got. When I was in the band, we had to march in Walmarts, convenient stores, and random office buildings just to raise money to go to football games. Clue no. 2: there wasn't an emphasis on the band. Who would have thought that through all the blood, sweat, and tears, I would be given the opportunity to rebuild the damage that was done because of the changeover in directors? So I did what I did best. Grind.

I combined the best of both worlds. With the best and most dedicated colleagues from my experiences at both colleges, we created the "Leaders of the New School." We would evolve this band into a musical and visually stimulating, entertaining, yet precise band of the future while preserve the true heart and soul of the band of the past. And it was happening.

I was told to go recruit and bring back a band. So I wrote a proposal for instruments. They were provided. I wrote a proposal for instruments; they were provided. I gave out every piece of money and more that I had to get quality musicians to return to the school, and they came. That was a task trying to convince students to come to a program that had a reputation for greatness but were no longer great. We planned and planned and rehearsed and brought in clinicians and hosted events and traveled and traveled and traveled. We battled the best in our conference, and we did great! Everyone was happy. The band program was back! In January or February 2008, the president announced that she would not be returning to the university. I knew then that we could be in a world of trouble. When the chief administrator changes, you will get either someone who understands or someone who has to be taught to understand the importance of not only the band but also the instrumental music at a college or university.

In the meantime, I was strategically planning the growth of the band, with hopes that someone would listen and understand that a band program with a budget of $150,000 for scholarships where a tuition of $22,000 per student is virtually impossible, not to mention an operational budget of $55,000 per year, including staff salaries. It doesn't take a rocket scientist to divide those numbers up. The band would never be over fifty members. I had four different supervisors in three semesters of working with the band. None of whom had experience with a band program. My proposal was juggled throughout the university. No one listened. I recruited my ass off, and as a result, 50 instrumentalists in 2007 turned into 110 in 2008. Everyone showed up for band camp! Time came to validate, and I gave just like I gave in 2007. I exceeded the budget. Everything went downhill from there. The operational budget was depleted in September.

Now this is my version of the story, so remember I am a little biased, but I have to disclose some information that is sensitive.

After I noticed that I was exceeding the budget, I contacted the administration. I was reprimanded but was given the opportunity to continue working. We had one trombone player that was short $2,000. The president told me, "You can take it out of your salary. Should we process the paperwork?" We played at every wine and cheese event that required jazz bands, two of which were in the middle of August during band camp. We traveled to a college out of state in North Carolina, and on the way up, a decision was made to postpone the game. We were already in North Carolina, but we even raised enough funds to stay the next day (in five hours), and we were told to return without playing the game. We were offered by the Barack Obama campaign to play for his rally. The president told me, "I don't care if Jesus Christ wants the band to play. He better be paying." In the meantime, we were being asked to play at every wine and cheese event that the university hosted.

Then we got hope. All departments were called in for a budget revision. This was my specialty. I presented the budget for us to get through the rest of the year, and it was approved. Supposedly . . . So we waited. January came. No updates. The band didn't travel at all. Then finally in February, about two weeks before the basketball tournament, funds were released, and we were able to participate in the tournament. The week immediately following the tournament, the music department's budget was frozen, and I was told that any other events that were planned for the year must be put on hold because of the overexpenditure in budget. Then I was told that there was no update that the band would have scholarships for 2009–2010. In the meantime, the band rehearsed and played at every home basketball game, rehearsing four days per week. Those of you who had never been a member of this band program must understand—we have *no* major for instrumental music. So our band was completely nonmusic majors. In addition, the band program consisted of only about fifty wind players. That means that the same people that are in pep band are in the jazz band and the wind ensemble. We would be practicing the pep band on Monday, concert band, jazz band, and indoor drum line on Tuesday and Thursday. Remember, all the same students! I was teaching two courses of music literature and an orientation class while doing private lessons, administrative work, marching band, symphonic, and other ensembles! I was the only faculty member in the department who worked with wind and percussion instrumentalists. I would see my family from 7:00 a.m. to 8:00 a.m., Monday through Friday, maybe Saturday nights, and all day on Sunday. I didn't complain. I just did the job.

The band students came together in a private meeting (I was impressed that it wasn't leaked to me). They decided to confront the administration about the allegations that we would not have band scholarships. The issue was immediately addressed, and the scholarships were restored. This created just enough positive morale for the students to prepare for the four-day inauguration and commencement that were scheduled for April. For this occasion, a mysterious amount of money showed up. The full band was in tuxedos; transportation and food were taken care of as well as a VIP room in Westin. Two weeks later was graduation. The cafeteria stopped serving students at lunch the day before graduation, forcing me to pay out of my pocket for breakfast and negotiating dinner with FDY. Two weeks later, I was called in for a meeting with the human resources, the president, and the dean.

On May 31, 2009, my contract will end and, as per the president of the university, will not be renewed for 2009–2010.

Now I would have never thought that the field of music could be this political. I was brought here to build a program. I made all the right moves to be successful. It really saddens me, but I will

31

move on. I feel for you, the students, and I feel for the university. I remain an advocate for the university, but I am not an advocate of the administration.

Guys, base your decision to stay on your love for the program. You pledged your allegiance to the band and school, not to me. No one knows what the administration has in store for you, so I can't speak either way. All I can say is I love each of you, staff and students. I and my family will be fine. God has a way of providing life lessons and opportunities for me. In the words of Puffy Combs, "What doesn't break you will make you." My intentions were in the interest of the band program, and I've learned in the last twenty-nine hours that my vision for the band was greater than my vision for the university. That would never work. No one can be successful under the conditions that I and the band program have been placed. To my potential bruhs, I say, "Keep striving." And to my sorors, I say, "Thanks for your service. Keep the band together." To the entire band, I say, "Good luck to you all and keep living by the motto: dedication, determination, and drive."

Musically yours,
Thurman D. Hollins

Chapter 9

FROM BARREN TO BEAUTIFUL (2009)

The summer of 2009 was one of my most difficult summers. I had worked so hard to build a program. I made a mistake and was displaced. I questioned my passion. I moped around the house for about three weeks. Then my phone rang. It was the president who hired me in 2007. She had retired but returned to work after being called to help out a university in Salisbury, North Carolina. She was friends with the president of the rival school across town. She said, "Thurman, there is a job open here, and I want you to apply for it."

"Yes, ma'am," I replied. I was interviewed for the position in June. I had a contract two weeks later. On July 6, I was moving in the office and received my first paycheck that next week. This was great! Well, that part was great. I was still a bit skeptical about working at a college again.

This new school traditionally had a great symphonic band, but over years, the tuition became higher, and it was difficult to maintain the program with very little funding. Even through the rough times, the administration at this school decided to bring a football program back. With the incorporation of football, a marching band became a want for the upper administration. This school only had a marching band for four years. Unfortunately, the band director who started the band passed away. And this was where my journey begins.

After being hired in July 2009, I did my best to recruit as many students as possible. I was very careful because I didn't want to exceed the budget. But I knew I wanted to at least have full instrumentation. I had just left a band of eighty musicians. From the tapes that I had reviewed of the band program, I counted around forty band members.

I called all my colleagues up and down the east coast. One in particular provided a very simple philosophy. "Treat them like they are big!" he said. What he meant was that I should apply the same standards and values expected from a large program to a smaller program. Our job is to instill good values, regardless of whether it's one kid or one hundred. That always stuck with me.

On the first day of band camp, I walked in the room and counted eleven wind players. It was the scariest day of my life. I walked out of the room for a moment to regain my composure. Flashes of my award-winning high school, my middle school of one hundred members, and my first collegiate band popped up in my head. All those were a distant memory. I began to question my abilities. I was scarred from my last position. I was scared to care again. Yes, I had a reputation for building great programs, but these kids cared nothing about that. They had just lost their hero—the previous band director. I needed to heal the band program. I thought about my colleague's words, said a short prayer, and did a "to the rear" and forward march into the band program to lead this band.

I had many frustrating days at this school, but I had some great musicians. This opportunity allowed me to slow down and focus on the needs of each player. This really tested my arranging and drill-writing abilities. I learned about "creative constraint" and finding out how to make things work when you have limited resources. I learned about having an open relationship with your supervisors. I learned that you have to put in work on and off the stage in order to build a music program. The program was growing, and I was growing with it. There was a strategic plan for growth, and the university was beginning to invest. Then the economy crashed.

During 2008–2010, around the beginning of the Obama administration, the country dealt with a housing crisis. Homes were foreclosing all over the United States. The technology wave had jobs closing down, and the federal government was pulling back funding for colleges while the price was rising. There was a trickle-down effect that happened in higher education. During those times, student enrollment decreased. At a small college of one thousand five hundred students, a decrease in three hundred students could turn a budget upside down. Apparently, the budget folks at that college didn't get the message until it was too late. They kept spending on a projected budget and ended up in serious debt. Scholarships were cut, and they were scheduling a furlough for the summer break. Though I loved my experience at that school, I knew that I had to seek other opportunities. I applied to many colleges and actually went on a few interviews. I guess that those opportunities weren't for me, but I was patient. I wasn't going to make any move that would mess up the stability of my family. I just knew that I had finally became confident enough and passionate enough to build a major program. I was ready.

One Friday after work, I got mysterious call from another university. This was totally surprising because, though the program was going through some tough times in terms of declining membership, they seemed to be okay. The caller informed me that they wanted a change in leadership. My exact words were "Call me once the position is open, and I'll consider talking to you about it."

You see, I had great mentors who told me to always be ethical. Though I didn't have a personal relationship with the current director there, I wasn't going to discuss the position while someone else was in it. When they let the director go, all hell broke loose. I understood that kind of backlash because it had already happened to me. Through my many experiences, I considered a few things before taking the job.

1. They were going to fill the position with somebody. Why not me?
2. The students needed someone who understood how to deal with the loss of a director.

3. My entire career was based on transitions.
4. I didn't have to move my family.
5. I had created a blueprint for success.

They announced me as the head director in mid-June around two weeks after letting the previous director and staff go. I was finishing my contract at my current school, but when the media got wind of it, they were calling my office around the clock. One news guy said, "Thurman Hollins is stepping into a hornet's nest." The students were petitioning for the return of the band director. I'm not sure if I downplayed how deep things were going to get, but I felt like I was ready.

Chapter 10

THE GRASS AIN'T ALWAYS GREENER (2014)

Day 1, I did what I always do—try to find the students. I got a roster and called every student on the list. Remember, the majority of the students did not want me there. Well, I couldn't really say that; they just preferred their previous director. But I called each one to make sure they heard my voice and knew when camp was taking place. I had managed to get a crew of students up to the band room to help with a project around day 3. I had a lot of equipment in my car, so I pulled my care through the band room's garage. About an hour after the students left (without helping more than ten minutes), the police came to the door. The students had called the police on me. They wanted my car out of "their" band room. I was sure they wanted me to leave with the car too. Then the "anonymous" letter came. In summary it said this:

> Thurman Hollins is hazing students. Thurman Hollins stole instruments from his last school. Thurman Hollins is stealing money. Thurman Hollins's wife reports to him, and that is nepotism. Thurman Hollins's staff doesn't have degrees. Thurman Hollins doesn't tune the band. Thurman

Hollins got fired from his job four years ago, and you
can read at this link what happened.

And then the anonymous calls to the auditors began. Every day,
someone called the auditor, claiming that all the allegations above
were true. This was not an overstatement. It began happening on a
daily basis. Then it went to every other day. Then it went to once a
week. Then it went to once per month. And right when I thought that
they were tired of calling, they made one final attempt. I guess out
of frustration, they actually left their name this time.

These were heavy allegations that were all found to be untrue.
You see, I learned that haters had one job, and it was to hate. It made
sense to me that the students and alumni didn't want me there, but it
didn't make sense to me that they would go to such lengths to get me
out. It seemed that they wanted the program to fail, and I was just
not good at failing. I was never so close to quitting, but that meant I
would fail. I could not let those haters win.

Through all this madness, I learned that I couldn't control what
others said about me, falsely reported about me, or even attempted
to do to me or my family. What I could control was how I operated.
I knew that I had a clean operation. They attempted to poke holes in
everything that they didn't understand, so that made work to make it
even more efficient. To tell the truth, I was *mad* as hell—so mad that
I began to write. What spawned out of my madness was a manual to
guide every band director who would ever take over a position. So
where the diary ends, the manual begins.

Part B

JOURNEY TO
SOUND LIVING

Introduction

The Business of Band: Why Do I Need a Manual for Organization and Operations?

Building a band program is like starting a business. Every start-up business should have a business model or plan to aid in navigation toward your intended destination. Let's call it a business GPS. Though there are many routes to get to the destination, we all would like to use the one with the least obstacles.

As band directors, we should want to travel the route that leads to a superior-sounding band program. Many times, the music is the easiest part of our job. The paperwork, administrative responsibilities, and daily student management can sometimes make it difficult to reach our desired musical outcome. I have found that having a program that operates smoothly offstage or on the sidelines is equally as important as having musicians who performs well on stage. Many directors just do not know how to effectively manage their organizations, and the information is not being taught in our schools of music.

This operational manual is your GPS. Over the last fifteen years, the procedures have been tested and refined to minimize your roadblocks and obstacles. This manual will help you transition into your newly acquired job and will solidify the procedures for future transitions in leadership. This particular manual does not deal with musical pedagogy. In fact, it assumes that you are a great musician and teacher while addressing many nonmusical aspects of the interworkings of a high school or collegiate band program. This manual is also highly recommended for aspiring music educators, first-year teachers, and seasoned directors seeking a written guide to aid in strategic planning and the "passing of the baton." This manual guides you from the contract signing through the initial meeting with the students. Of course, situations arise that may require modification or update of the procedures, but it is better to have a map to a location and make a decision to find a better route than to not have map and navigate through the wilderness, hoping that you will make it to the destination. Your destination has been entered, so let's start the journey.

Chapter 1

THE TRANSITION AND THE PROCESS OF PASSING AND RECEIVING THE BATON

Assuming a leadership position like that of a band director can initially be a very exciting experience. The multitude of congratulatory praises, statements of support, and good wishes all serve as motivation to the director. However, with any type of change in leadership, it can also be very emotional to the individuals who are accustomed to certain practices, cultures, and traditions. In an ideal situation, the previous leader is available to provide guidance to the new director. This can set up the new director for a smooth transition if the previous director introduces the new leaders to students, parents, and supportive entities throughout the community, especially if the previous director was well respected. This serves as an unofficial endorsement of the transition in leadership.

My first job out of college was pretty smooth. I met the previous director who had only been there one year. I had discussions with the students and parents prior to being hired. The school principal wanted youthful energy, and they took a chance on me. When I took over the middle school, the previous director was transferring within the system, so he was able to provide some background about the position that helped me get started. When I took over the first collegiate band, it was also a smooth transition because I had already established rapport with the students, staff, and alumni because I served as the assistant director first. In many cases, this situation is highly unlikely.

As I took over my second collegiate job, the transition was different. This band program was young and only had one previous marching band director. He abruptly died during his fourth year leading the band. So when I took over, the students were very hesitant. They had to heal from losing their past director. I decided that I needed to work with the student leaders first. We analyzed the strengths and weaknesses of the band and set some goals. This allowed them to understand that they would have some level of input into the future of the band program. Once that trust was established, we could move forward.

The transition into my third collegiate job was basically a hornet's nest. The administration decided they wanted to "go into a different direction." That was the new code for "we're not renewing your contract." That director had built the program for over ten years into a phenomenal program. He was loved by the students and alumni but was dismissed. In order to move forward with this program, I would have to implement some of the same concepts as before. They had to trust that I was taking care of them if we were going to be able to move forward. I decided to not only work with the leaders first but also make a phone call to each incoming member to introduce myself and make sure they had all the necessary information to continue with the program. As the leaders became more comfortable, they shared that information with their peers. While this helped some, their healing process was so deep that the transition process lasted for another three years.

Midsummer transitions in leadership or abrupt midyear changes don't allow for a smooth passing of the baton. In these situations, students have feelings of uncertainty about rules and policies, organizational procedures, and overall direction of the program. Some parental support organizations will naturally be uneasy and possibly assume unassigned responsibilities or roles. Sometimes rough transitions and abrupt changes will create and magnify an allegiance to the previous director simply because of the discomfort of the "possibility" of change.

Most of these scenarios happen with good intentions (mostly, intentions of keeping things consistent) but can cause more confusion for the director in the future (especially if the new director makes adjustments to enhance the procedures). The new director should simply remain calm and provide clear and concise directions, roles, and responsibilities to all parties. This transitional point calls for the need to have standard operational procedures.

Chapter 2

GETTING STARTED: I SIGNED MY CONTRACT, NOW WHAT?

During your first week, it is imperative that you take inventory. Take photos of the condition of your instruments. If you have some type of online system such as Charms to help, get it going. This is a great time to incorporate your parent organizations or a small group of band volunteers. You can build rapport while working on this task.

Inventory is very important because you are responsible for everything that the band has. The school will probably check it if you decide to take another job, and you want to make sure you keep impeccable records. Conducting an inventory will also let you assess the true conditions of the band program so that you can create a preliminary report. Submit that report to your supervisors as soon as possible so that they will be award about the needs of the program. Never be afraid to provide information about program needs to your administration. Most administrators have no clue about what it takes to operate a successful ensemble, so it is your job to inform them and advocate for your program. You never know what kind of support exists for your program, but if you don't communicate those needs, you are guaranteed to get nothing.

I did a preliminary report for my first job and received $40,000 from the county for the purchase of new equipment. After providing a preliminary report to the president of my first collegiate job, the president found $250,000. She gave me a week to spend it all. I did just that. The program was in such bad shape, I had to buy chairs, stands, podiums, uniforms, and instruments. I showed the current need by hosting the inventory, assessing needed repairs, and showing the current state of the equipment. We got the money and had a great season.

Outside of inventory and preliminary report, you must find out the "who" and "what" of the school or university. The "who" refers to the important individuals you need to know in order to effectively do your job. They can include your supervisors, budget approvers, sponsors, support staff, campus partners, cafeteria workers, and custodial staff. You must establish a working relationship with those individuals as soon as possible.

The "what" refers to the type of operating system the school uses to process paperwork, make purchases, reserve facilities, request leave, and input grades and attendance. Schedule your trainings as soon as possible. These things will help you get your groundwork quickly done so you can get back focused on the music. Below are some steps that you should implement upon higher:

1. See your supervisor for the following: office space, retrieve email, phone and computer access, proper mailing address, and copy access.

2. Do an *inventory* immediately. Take pictures. Compare previous inventory list with what is actually physically present. Document your findings and report them to your supervisor.

3. Create a *preliminary report* that addresses the current state of the program. The report should address the immediate needs of the program: large inventory (uniforms and instruments), instructional supplies (music, technology, books, and educational resources), staffing, and any budget concerns. It is recommended that you get professional assistance to assess these items and provide quotes of needed equipment.

4. Set up the following trainings as soon as possible: budget training, room reservation, intranet, and grades submission.

5. For school or university performance expectations, set up a meeting with the following campus leaders: dean or arts supervisor, music department chair, athletics, student affairs, Greek life, alumni affairs, homecoming committee.

6. Prepare a phone and email roster with a main contact for the following departments: president or chancellor or principal, assistants or vice presidents, dean or arts supervisor, music department, budgeting or financial aid, admissions or counselors, student affairs, central receiving, residence life, dining services, travel, accounts payable, facilities services, and foundation or sponsorship offices.

7. Collect previous band rosters and contact information. Create a system for contacting all students (phone, email, and social media).

8. Have a casual meeting or lunch with the following local partners: band boosters, area music directors, county music supervisor, arts organizations, state band directors association, local music vendors, and local media representatives (newspaper, radio, and television).

Other contacts will be made throughout the year, mostly at the other party's request. Keep a running list of contacts. Build relationships and send thank-you notes.

Chapter 3

BAND STAFF ORGANIZATIONAL MODEL

The following chapter includes job descriptions for the band-staff instructional positions, noninstructional positions, student staff, and support-staff positions. It is of great importance that we begin to implement these positions to provide individualized instruction, supervision, student management, and assistance to the director of bands. The purpose is to provide further insight into the responsibilities associated with the operations of a collegiate marching band program.

As evident in the numerous positions and committees, the responsibilities associated with marching band operations are far too great for one person to accomplish, but with a team and this organizational model, individuals can be accountable for the work to be done. On a football coaching staff, you have the head coach, assistant coaches, offensive and defensive coordinators, water crew, and athletic trainers. However, only eleven players can be on the field at a time. The same type of staffing is needed for a marching band program, especially since all members perform pregame, during the game, halftime, and postgame. Charts are included to visually show how the band functions.

In many cases, the school district or institution does not have funding for additional instructional positions. Don't get discouraged. Use this opportunity to train student leaders to handle simple responsibilities that can be of assistance to you. Empowering the student instills a feeling of responsibility for the band's success. It also provides some much needed life skills that are transferable outside of the ensemble, such as teamwork, management skills, conflict resolution, and accountability. Some instructional positions can be filled by qualified volunteers who are approved by your institution. Make sure you have clear expectations and roles for those individuals if they are volunteers. Additionally, your instructional vision must be provided to all person's involved in teaching. Show plans, music, field show design, visuals, and choreography must be thoroughly planned, and meetings must take place.

Before doing any work, make sure you have established clear roles for both instructional staff and support staff. Depending on the established practices of the previous directors, you may need to change preestablished roles. Sometimes this will upset your staff, but you have to be comfortable with your help. Write those responsibilities down so that there is no confusion. When I taught high school, we had band boosters. Because there had been no stability in directors, the parents began assuming roles that were beyond their responsibility. They wanted to establish schedules, make suggestions for uniforms, and deal with logistical procedures. Because I was young enough to be their child, they felt that they could say or do anything to me. I had to shut it down.

I remember we were leaving for the Christmas parade in Downtown Richmond. As I always did, I was the last out of the band room and the final person to load the buses. So after locking up the room as usual, I walked to the parking lot, only to notice that the band was gone. One of the parents told the drivers that the band was ready to go, and the driver actually left me. Cell phones weren't that popular at the time, so I had no communication with the parent or driver. Needless to say, after driving to the parade site, I let both the parents and the drivers have it.

Another time, the boosters decided to call a private meeting without me at a public library. I found out and crashed the meeting. I gave them the opportunity to express anything that they wanted up close and personal, but the room went silent. I proceeded to tell them that the organization only functions at the pleasure of the director. Anything outside of support for my initiatives to build the program and teach the students should not be discussed. After that meeting, the organization got smaller, but I was happy with how much we developed.

At my first college, we had a staff of sixteen people. On paper, everyone had very specific roles, but things still didn't totally work out because we were too close as friends and the staff who were alums were not mature enough to ensure a staff-student divide. They wanted to hang out in the office when it was actually time to work. At times, they would forget that the band trips were for the student experience and we had work to do. Though I was happy with the band's musical output, I was not happy at the operations. I quickly learned that I had to establish a line between my friendly relationship with the staff and my professional relationship with the staff. So I wrote down each staff member's responsibilities in rehearsals, at performances, and during travel. I also did a midyear assessment of their progress. I had minimal issues once those lines weren't blurred anymore. We established clear communication of responsibilities and my expectations. It felt better and the operations worked out better.

The organizational model provided is merely a goal for band programs. More importantly are the responsibilities of each position. Use the responsibility section to create your own organizational model based on your available personnel. Designate the responsibilities to your available personnel based on their skill set. Use your judgment and continuously assess their productivity. The main thing is to *effectively get the job done.*

Band Staff

Job Descriptions

*Instructional Positions
Director of Bands
Assistant Band Director
Percussion Instructor / Rehearsal Assistant
Flag Instructor
Dance Instructor
Leadership Coordinator / Fitness Trainer

*Noninstructional Positions
Administrative Assistant
Music Librarian
Instrument/Uniform Room Maintenance
Announcer

Student Staff / Work Study Positions
Field and Game Day Crew
Student Arranger
Office Assistant

Support Staff
Band Photographer/Videographer
Band Webmaster
Student Staff
Work Study
Alumni Band President

Committees
Uniform Room
Instrument Room
Arranging
Dance/Show Planning

*Instructional and Noninstructional positions are paid positions.

Instructional Positions

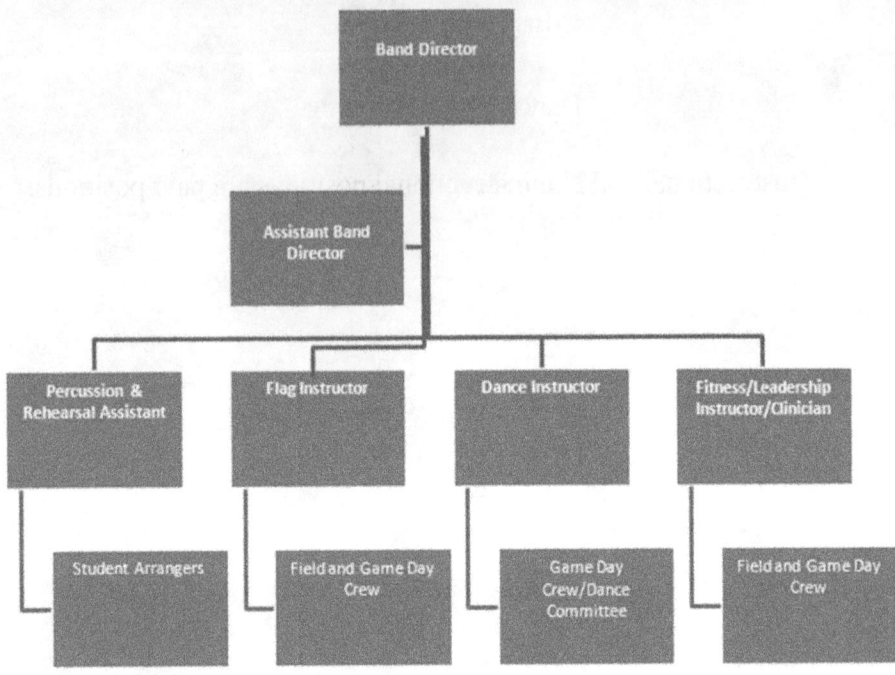

Noninstructional Positions

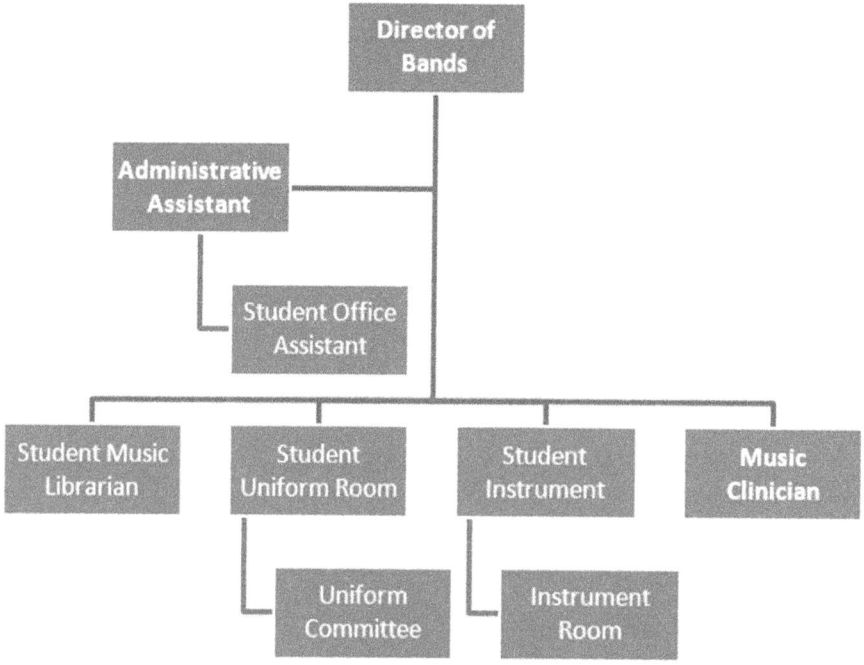

Bold = Paid Staff

Performing Members Organizational Chart

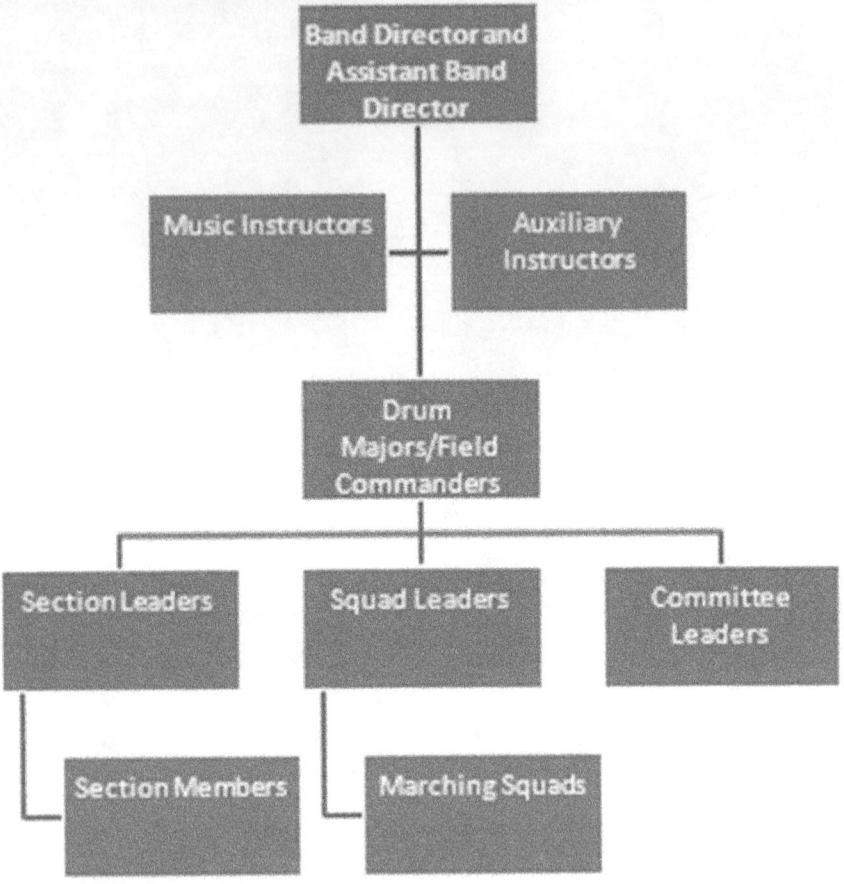

See next pages for job descriptions.

Assistant Director of Bands

Division: Bands
Department: Music Department
Wage:
Reports to: Director of Bands

Qualifications: An earned bachelor's degree in music education from an accredited university and a valid teaching license with required endorsements for music are required. Candidate must demonstrate the ability to teach a wide range of skill levels and must be committed and dedicated to teaching and managing a large group of students.

Special Knowledge and Skills

Knowledge of content
General knowledge of curriculum and instruction
Music arrangement and composition
Drill writing

Major Responsibilities and Duties

Instructional Management

1. Monitor instruction of music on a continuous and systematic basis.

   a. In collaboration with the director of bands, plan, coordinate resources, and actively participate in the summer marching band.
   b. In collaboration with the director of bands, plan, coordinate resources, and actively participate in all rehearsals during the school year.
   c. Actively participate in all sectional music rehearsals during the school year.
   d. Attend all marching band performances during the year.

e. e. Serve as the pep band sponsor in the spring semester.

f. Conduct small ensemble and assist with wind-ensemble rehearsals in the spring semester.

g. Develop, plan, coordinate resources, and develop specific areas of the band program as designated by the director of bands.

h. Administer and coordinate instrumental music instruction with the director of bands.

2. Work closely with and assist the director of bands and campus administrators in dealing with instructional issues of the department of instrumental music.

    a. Maintain communication with the director of bands regarding all facets pertaining to the department of bands.

    b. Through the director of bands, or directly as the situation warrants, keep campus administrators informed of all facets and events pertaining to the band program.

3. Present the subject matter according to the guidelines, policies, and regulations established by the school or university.

Student Growth and Development

1. Assist students in analyzing and improving methods and habits of study.

2. Consistently assess student progress through formal and informal testing.

3. Provide a positive role model for the students.

Classroom Management and Organization

1. Create a classroom environment conducive to learning and appropriate to the physical, social, and emotional development of students.

2. Assist in the selection of books, equipment, and other instructional materials.
3. Work closely with the director of bands in providing music facilities and equipment that are conducive to the development of the music students and the music program.
4. Maintain an accurate record of all music and instruments.

Communication

1. Maintain a professional relationship with faculty, staff, students, and the community.
2. Use acceptable communication skills to accurately and clearly present information.

Professional Development

1. Participate in the district, state, and national conferences for instrumental music.
2. Demonstrate interest and initiative in professional improvement.
3. Demonstrate behavior that is professional, ethical, and responsible.

Percussion Instructor / Rehearsal Assistant

Reports to: Director of Bands
Dates:
Salary:

Job Description

1. Conduct or facilitate sectional rehearsals for the percussion section.
2. Arrange or compose performance material for field shows, parades, and any other performances at the request of the director of bands and assist with full band rehearsals.
3. Conduct placement auditions for the percussion section.
4. Facilitate individual percussion instruction (new personnel).
5. Communicate instrumental needs of the percussion section to the director or the assistant director of bands.
6. Teach and enhance rudimental playing ability, discipline, posture, technique, sound cohesion, general effect, and creativity.

Requirements

1. Attend midday and evening rehearsals during summer band camp. See the director of bands for scheduling.
2. Attend at least three sectional rehearsals per week.
3. Attend all band performances.
4. Conduct rehearsals for summer band camp. See the director of bands for scheduling.

Band Assistant / Flag Instructor

Reports to: Director of Bands
Dates:
Salary:

Job Description

1. Conduct or facilitate sectional rehearsals for the flag section.
2. Coordinate flag choreography for field shows, parades, and any other performances at the request of the director or the assistant director of bands.
3. Communicate the needs of the flag section to the director or assistant director of bands.
4. Recruit for the flag section.
5. Conduct auditions for section leader recommendations and new members.

Requirements

1. Attend midday and evening rehearsals during summer band camp. See the director of bands for scheduling.
2. Attend at least three sectional rehearsals per week.
3. Attend all band performances.
4. Conduct rehearsals for summer band camp. See the director of bands for scheduling.

Band Assistant / Dance Instructor

Reports to: Director of Bands
Dates:
Salary:

Job Description

1. Conduct or facilitate sectional rehearsals for the dance section.
2. Coordinate dance choreography for field shows, parades, and any other performances at the request of the director or assistant director of bands.
3. Communicate the needs of the dance section to the director or assistant director of bands.
4. Coordinate separate performances for the dance section.
5. Be the spring-dance line coordinator.
6. Recruit for the dance section.
7. Conduct auditions and section leader recommendations.

Requirements

1. Attend midday and evening rehearsals during the summer band camp. See the director of bands for scheduling.
2. Attend at least three sectional rehearsals per week.
3. Attend all band performances.
4. Conduct rehearsals for the summer band camp. See the director of bands for scheduling.

Drum Major / Fitness Coordinator

Reports to: Director of Bands
Dates:
Salary:

Job Description

1. Conduct a comprehensive fitness program that encompasses cardiovascular training and strength building.
2. Teach and enhance marching techniques.
3. Conduct or facilitate sectional rehearsals for the drum majors
4. Coordinate the drum-major choreography for field shows, parades, and any other performances at the request of the director or assistant director of bands.
5. Teach and model leadership qualities to drum majors and section leaders.
6. Conduct team-building exercises for the full band.
7. Coordinate drum major tryouts

Requirements

1. Attend morning and evening sessions of band camp.
2. Attend *all* band performances. See the director of bands for scheduling.

Administrative Assistant

Reports to: Director of Bands
Dates:
Salary:

Job Description

Communicate with the director of bands and other instructors to complete the following:

1. Type or copy any communication to the band staff and students.
2. Distribute, collect, and file student forms (i.e., information, medical ECT).
3. Proofread publications and advertising materials for the band.
4. Submit requisitions, orders, and facility-use request to appropriate university officials.
5. Organize music and scores for the use of music instructors and band students.
6. Coordinate hospitality for staff meetings, band events, and visitors.
7. Conduct mailings of student recruitment packets, homecoming, band day, and other band events at the discretion of the director or assistant director of bands.

Requirements

1. Work twenty to twenty-five hours per week. Additional meetings required at the discretion of the director of bands.
2. Attend band performances.
3. Attend summer band camp. See the director of bands for scheduling.

Student Music Librarian

Reports to: Director of Bands
Dates:
Salary:

Job Description

1. Organize music and scores for the use of music instructors and band students.
2. Distribute music for rehearsals.
3. Work with the assistant director of bands, assistant instructor of music, and student arrangers to preserve the hardcopies and electronic versions of musical scores.
4. Organize a working filing system for the music library.
5. Organize the student music library committee.

Requirements

1. Attend at least two rehearsals per week. Additional meetings required at the discretion of the director of bands.
2. Attend band performance.
3. Attend summer band camp. See the director of bands for scheduling.

Student Uniform and Instrumental Managers

Reports to: Director of Bands
Dates:
Salary:

Job Description

1. Conduct preseason and postseason inventory of instrument and uniform rooms.
2. Facilitate the check-in and checkout of equipment and uniforms.
3. Communicate and enforce care and maintenance requirements for band students.
4. Report needed repairs on instruments and uniforms.
5. Communicate with cleaners and music stores for cleaning and maintaining instruments and uniforms.
6. Organize and facilitate the student uniform committee.
7. Communicate instrumental and uniform needs to the director or assistant director of bands.

Requirements

1. Attend at least one rehearsal per week. Additional meetings required at the discretion of the director of bands.
2. Attend band performances.
3. Attend summer band camp. See the director of bands for scheduling.

Announcer

Reports to: Director of Bands
Dates:
Salary:

Job Description

1. Coordinate show announcements for all band performances.
2. Submit show announcements to the director of bands.
3. Communicate and preserve historical data of the band program.
4. Organize historical data for band handbook updates.

Requirements

1. Attend or conduct at least two rehearsals per week.
2. Attend *all* band performances.
3. Attend summer band camp. See the director of bands for scheduling.

Chapter 4

RECRUITMENT AND RETENTION: HOW DO I FIND THE STUDENTS BEFORE SCHOOL STARTS?

While recruitment is an ongoing process, in the spring semester, light performance demands allow directors, staff, and the student recruitment team the time to organize, plan, market, and target. Many times during short transitions, directors do not have time to take trips to feeder schools to find students. In this case, the director should begin by using the admissions office, guidance counselors, and class rosters. The next step should be to contact student leaders and volunteers in an attempt to reach students. Create a phone tree to contact sectional members to acquire appropriate contact information. It is imperative to find a consistent means of communicating with the band members. Webpages, email, social media, and phone trees are all good ways to establish clear communication. This reduces confusion and misinformation. Finally, a meeting should be scheduled to formally reiterate any policies, discuss upcoming rehearsals and performances, and discuss any fees.

This meeting is your first impression on your students, parents, and supporters. Make sure all technology is ready, and you are very organized. Be confident, but if questions are asked that you need more time to address, take a running list and inform them of when you will provide more clarifications.

I was hired at my first college on July 6, so I had to move first to find the band and recruit new students. Finding the old roster was pretty easy, but the program only had about twenty returning students. So I knew I had to work fast to find any new students that may have interest in joining the program. I began with an online marketing campaign. I sent emails to band directors, and I created a Facebook page and posted flyers and preregistration links for students to sign up for auditions. I also found out when the school's summer orientations or open houses would take place. I made contact with the event coordinator so that the initiative to build the band would be incorporated into the itinerary. In any business model, you must market your product. The main idea is to make sure people know that you are selling something so they will know that the product is available for purchase. In this case, you're selling an educational experience. Market the experience, build your database, and contact the students as soon as possible. It can get tricky, especially when you are working against time. But once you set up the system, it can be repeated each year.

Sometimes earlier transitions provide more time to recruit for the beginning of the season. The following are steps to recruit effectively for your band:

1. Identify personnel deficiencies in the wind ensemble *first*. This is the top ensemble and the core of all other ensembles. This ensemble is where you will find your best musicians. If at all possible, target potential music majors. Identify deficiencies in the marching ensemble next. Poll feeder-school directors to see if they have students who could potentially fill those particular positions.

2. Recruitment materials should be updated and ready for distribution. The recruitment packet includes the university admission's information, a student information form, the audition's information, and a director's recommendation form. The recruitment display is a board that is used for fairs and community events that visually shows the band program in action. Digital slide shows and videos enhance the display.

3. A running database of recruits will be kept during the recruitment season. Following a recruitment trip, student information forms should be submitted to the director of bands, staff, and student recruitment team leader.

4. The band director will keep a current database of feeder-school directors for the purpose of targeted recruitment and consistent networking.

5. Planned school visits and performances will occur during the spring semester. The best recruitment endeavors are live performances. Based on budget, the band program should allow a minimum of one performance and three school visits per month.

6. An on-campus "open house" event should be annually planned. This will serve as an opportunity to market the campus and band program and to conduct auditions.

7. To ensure good customer service and effective correspondence, keep campus partners and supervisors informed of your endeavors. They include the music department chair, admissions representative, financial aid representative, and residence life. Keep an updated database of phone numbers and emails for these individuals.

Chapter 5

AUDITIONS AND SCHOLARSHIPS: GETTING TO KNOW YOUR PERFORMERS

It is imperative that you assess the playing ability of the students in your ensemble. Auditioning students allow you not only to determine the proficiency level of your students but also to teach your students how to prepare for future tryouts. Auditions can be individually held prior to beginning the ensemble (which is the preferred method), or (if time doesn't permit) you can conduct them during your first ensemble meetings.

At one school, the transition was so sensitive that I chose to not audition the students. I didn't want them to feel overwhelmed with the emotions of dealing with a new director and new policies. Instead, I incorporated weekly checkoff auditions on the performance material. This allowed me the opportunity to identify errors and correct them without the ranking system. After the semester was over, I auditioned each student individually for the other ensembles. While this worked out in this situation, I would probably prefer auditioning students for placement in every ensemble. It humbles the overconfident student, and it builds confidence in the weaker students. It also reinforces the chain of command and the student-teacher relationship. This is your group, and they must audition to be in your group.

The audition process is twofold. Auditions are conducted for ensembles or music department admission or placement and for college scholarship awards. The process for auditioning is listed below.

1. The student should prepare at least one etude, *all* major scales, chromatic scale, and sight-reading. The number of scales and level of etude can vary, depending on the level of band (intermediate or advanced).
2. The director of bands should prepare audition sheets, sight-reading materials, scholarship logs, and scholarship contracts.
3. Students interested in auditioning should either register to attend the advertised open audition or call the director of bands or staff member to schedule an audition. Sometimes the director will schedule auditions during off-campus recruitment events. Video auditions are accepted in cases in which the student is out of state or the director is unavailable to conduct the audition.
4. If a student qualifies for a scholarship, a scholarship letter of recommendation is distributed to the student. The recommendation is based solely on the audition and can be adjusted once the financial-aid award is processed. Once the financial-aid award is processed, a final amount is determined, and the student will receive a scholarship contract from the director. Both the student and director will sign the contract. Scholarship dispersals will take place once per month, beginning in April 15 and ending on August 15. It is highly recommended that the scholarships are distributed to the music majors and concert-jazz ensemble musicians first. Then fill the marching band out with the best players in the sections with the greatest areas of need.

Chapter 6:

BAND CAMP: PREPARATION FOR A GREAT FALL

There are so many tasks to be completed so that you can prepare for the arrival of the students. You must make sure you reserve your rehearsal areas, determine your housing requirements and meal options, make instructional plans, establish your staff, and create a budget for your camp. My general rule is to think about the basic needs: rehearsal space, instructional needs, equipment, housing, and food. After you establish all these things, create an informational packet for your parents and students, which includes important deadlines and any fees that you may have.

Sometimes your facility managers can be very territorial. You must establish a great working relationship with those individuals and make sure your students respect their areas by keeping them clean and secure. Always double-check your reservations for accuracy and send reminders to the building managers prior to your event. This will ensure that the spaces are unlocked and set up for your needs. Always check the location at least twenty-four hours in advance, especially if you're using any type of technology for your rehearsal. Just as you have a lesson plan for the students, you must make sure your space is just as prepared as your instructional plan.

Everything comes with a cost. It is your job to determine how to get it paid and who is going to pay it. Many programs use a "fair share" concept where expenses are totally paid by the student, but they can work them off by doing fund-raisers. Some programs determine the budget and seek out sponsors to take care of certain items. For instance, the boosters may commit to paying for three out of five of the camp meals, and a corporate sponsor can pay for the other half. If you have a budget, the band program or music department can pay for the summer instrument repairs, while camp supplies can be covered through student fees. The idea is to keep the camp expenses as low as possible so that it doesn't affect other line items, such as travel.

A successful band camp leads to a successful season and successful ensemble. Get your plans solidified and advertised as early as possible so that your students and parents will be aware of all upcoming events. Below are some steps to help you prepare for your preseason band camp.

1. A band camp proposal should be submitted to all supervisors in March of the previous spring semester. The proposal should include the dates and budget for camp.
2. The band camp budget should include staffing, housing, meals, educational resources, supplies, summer performance attire, printing, uniforms, and equipment.
3. The following campus partners should be contacted for band camp:
   a. *Staffing:* music department chair and other supervisors (Personnel requisition may be required.)
   b. *Dorms*: residence life (List of students and ID numbers are required. The housing deposit and application must be received.)
   c. *Registration*: registrar or counselor (All students must be a full-time student and registered for the band class prior to reporting to band camp. The band director must verify

that students remain on the class roster in order to remain an active member in full standing.)

d. *Meals*: dining service provider (List of students and ID numbers are required.)

e. *Summer attire:* approved vendor (Quote and purchase Order, or PO, are required.)

f. *Uniforms:* approved vendor (Quote and PO are required for repairs and replacement orders. The directors and staff must determine the amount and sizes of uniforms that are needed for the season. A uniform fitting should occur to sizes. If uniforms are beyond repair or demand exceeds the inventory, then replacement uniforms should be purchased.)

g. *gInstrumental equipment:* approved vendor (Quote and PO are required for repairs and replacement orders. The director has to determine which instrument is needed for the season. A repair assessment should be matched with potential instrumentation to determine which instrument is needed for the season. If instruments are beyond repair or demand exceeds the inventory, then the instruments should be rented or purchased.)

h. *Printing music and forms*: copy center or school copy procedures

4. Once approved, the band camp should be advertised to potential students, and the returning students should be notified.

5. During the month of June, a band camp packet will be advertised to all returning and potential band members and will be posted on the website. The packet will include the band camp schedule, performance schedule, fees, dorm information, special instrument requirements, and ensemble expectations. All students should register for camp by July 15.

6. The staff should begin planning the instruction for band camp in July. Staff retreats will take place once per week to

determine the first show requirements. Rehearsal plans will be completed based on camp schedule.

7. Other logistical items and campus contacts for band camp are listed below.

   a. Campus security and housekeeping facilities should be notified of the band itinerary.

   b. Rehearsal spaces should be reserved.

      Areas: athletics and music department supervisor

      Full band: reserve field

      Auxiliary rehearsals: gymnasium, auditorium, or dance studio, *Music rehearsals or sectionals:* music ensemble rooms or classroom

8. The welcome meeting should be planned to orient students on the rules and regulations of the campus and band camp.

   a. The panel should include the band staff and student leaders. Special invitations to speak should be sent to the principal, assistant principal, dean of CAS, vice chancellor of student affairs, music department chair, campus security, and the student health center.

   b. Forms for the "welcome meeting" include health or physical form, liability form, band camp registration, band camp itinerary, instrument checkout band handbook, travel agreement, and conflict form.

Chapter 7

TRAVEL: HOW DO
WE GET THERE?

Being afforded the opportunity to travel is one of the earned opportunities of participating in the band. Traveling becomes a marketing tool for the purpose of recruitment, and it also serves as a motivational aspect in preparation for the events. Travel is determined mainly by the allotted budget. However, certain performances are deemed important for public-relations opportunities, and they increase visibility and marketing potential for the university, at large.

Schools interpret band travel in different ways. Many schools feel that if the team is traveling, the band should be traveling. Some schools allow the band director to decide when and where the band will travel. Some schools don't allow the band to travel, or they travel only if they raise the funds to do so. As a director, you should base your travel plans in a balanced manner. Factors should include educational opportunity, athletic-team support, recruitment opportunity, public-relations or fund-raising opportunity, community service, and budget.

You cannot have too many educational opportunities, so those should be factored in first. However, if you only travel to football games, your student will miss out on opportunities to serve the community. If you only look for public-relations or fund-raising opportunities, you become sort of a circus band, and your students can begin to feel used.

To plan a balanced trip, it is probably cost effective and just downright smart to combine these things to create an awesome experience for your program. If you are traveling to a game, stop on the way to do some type of school or community performance. This could serve as a rehearsal for the larger performance. Seek out many opportunities in whatever area where you are traveling. Remember, the bus is already paid for, so get your money's worth. Here are some steps to assist with your travel plans:

1. If budget allows, determine dates, transportation, meals, and housing (if applicable).
2. Complete an itinerary based on the packing time, travel time, performance prep, meals, and return time.
3. The following entities should be contacted for travel:
   a. *Transportation:* travel office (Quote from an approved vendor and a PO or a request from a school- or university-owned vehicle via the transportation office. The itinerary should be sent to the driver.)
   b. *Meals:* travel office (Travel request and list of students and ID numbers are required. Meal destinations and funding source should be determined prior to the trip.)
   c. *Hotels:* travel office (Travel request, quote from approved hotel, room assignment, and a list of students and ID numbers are required. Check the hotel's check policy. Funding source should be determined prior to the trip.)
   d. *Certification:* Students must be in good academic standing in order to travel. Also, a written excuse should be generated by the director to the music department chair and endorsed by the CAS dean or supervising principal.
4. A student travel committee will be established to assist with the loading and unloading of equipment. The committee will

meet with the director of bands prior to the trip to establish the packing plan.

5. The packing plan should include instructions about where to place the following: bus roster with students' names, medical information, uniform accessory box, repair box, field equipment, wind instruments, percussion instruments, coolers, and snacks. Always keep a copy of *all* medical forms on each bus.

6. If meals or snacks from the dining hall are required, the travel committee is responsible for acquiring and distributing those meals.

7. A travel meeting should take place to discuss bus and hotel decorum, the itinerary, attire, rules, and consequences. *Behavior agreements* should be read and signed by all students and parents prior to the trip.

Chapter 8

SUPPORT ORGANIZATIONS: EXTENDING THE TEAM

Having a solid support staff is very important. You want your ensemble to operate like a well-oiled machine. You *must* make sure each person exactly knows what their role is in rehearsal, on performance day, and while traveling. In the beginning, you may need to call meetings to make sure all things are covered. Once it becomes practice, you can probably choose a chief of staff to follow up with the committee leaders.

Since you will be assigning the personnel, you have to determine whether the positions should be assigned to a student on work study or to a parent volunteer or booster. You may want to create an application or advertise the position in a way that explains the roles and your expectations of the position. Whether paid or not, the job needs to be done. And it must be correctly done in order to work. Remember, when the roles are not completely established, it may lead to confusion and a terrible work environment.

If it is a collegiate band booster or parent organization, make sure you assign a specific job to the organization. It should be to find financial support for the organization, but if you are short personnel, you may want to assign those volunteers in supervisory positions. They can be leaders of the student committees to help mentor and guide them through completing the tasks. Communicate with all support staff members on a weekly basis to ensure things are getting done in an effective manner. All machines require regular maintenance to make sure all parts are correctly running. It is the same with your staff. Be the boss. Communicate your needs, set your committees, designate responsibilities, hold those individuals accountable, assess effectiveness, and provide feedback. This will keep things smoothly flowing. Below are some examples of committees and their responsibilities.

Student Staff or Work Study Positions

Field and Game Day Crew

Responsibilities include but are not limited to loading and unloading equipment from the bus, securing performance locations in the stands for the band, ensuring equipment is in place on the field for rehearsals and performances, running auxiliary equipment during shows, filling water coolers prior to rehearsals, dispersing water, and assisting the director of bands for special events.

Student Arranger

Responsibilities include but are not limited to working with the director of bands, student leaders, and show planning committee to develop instrumental arrangements for field shows.

Office Assistant

Responsibilities include but are not limited to taking roll at all rehearsals and performances, leading the student recruitment team with the management of recruitment materials, and providing assistance to the band's administrative assistant.

Committees

Uniform and Instrument Room

Assists the uniform and instrument maintenance leader with the inventory, cleaning, organization, fitting, and dispersal of band uniforms.

Leadership

Consists of the drum majors and section leaders.

Dance or Show Planning

Coordinates band choreography for field shows, parades, and any other performances at the request of the director or assistant director of bands; coordinates popular music and choreography for field shows and stands; conducts or facilitate sectional rehearsals for the dance committee; and communicates musical needs to the student arrangers or the director of bands.

Recruitment

Accompanies band staff with recruitment endeavors and work with the office assistant in organizing recruitment information, call logs, and mailings.

The members of band in Greek organizations usually serve as the leaders of the committees and hold the student staff positions.

Support Staff

Band Photographer or Videographer
Documents rehearsals and performances for school or university public relations, marketing, and branding of the program.

Band Webmaster
Creates and maintains the website for band program

Alumni Band President or Alumni Liaison
Coordinates fundraisers for the organization, events in support of the current band, and alumni band activities for homecoming; and communicates all activities to the director of bands.

Band Booster
Provides financial support to the band program based on the projected goals provided by the band director. Can provide the personal support needed for committees above as recommended by the director of bands.

Chapter 9

STUDENT ARRIVAL: DAY 1 PROCEDURES

Prior to meeting with the entire ensembles, it is very important that you meet with the student leaders of the program. Change is uncomfortable, so it is better to just dive in those difficult conversations. During these sessions, you should allow the students to self-assess using the SWOT (strengths, weaknesses, opportunities, threats) analysis. SWOT will allow the students to take a comprehensive look at the program and set goals for improvement. It also clarifies their role in achieving the goals.

The leadership camp is also designed to review all the introductory materials with the leaders. The leadership sessions should contain the following:

1. SWOT Analysis
2. Principles of Musicianship
3. Calisthenics and Fundamentals of Drill
4. Team-Building Exercises
5. Band Culture, Traditions, and Past Practices
6. Sectional Management Tips and Conflict Resolution
7. Daily Rules, Operations, and Procedures
8. Director's Rules and Expectations

9. Overview of the Future Schedule

10. Student and Director's Goals for the Year

Your leaders should be able to handle peer group activities like sectionals. They should also be able to reinforce materials covered by the instructors without direct supervision. As instructor or directors, we should be "directing," and student leaders should be "leading." With a well-planned itinerary, you should be able to cover the basics of leadership. Meetings should periodically take place to provide further guidance and check sectional progress. Always take a moment to rotate and observe your leader in sectionals. Take notes so that you can provide feedback. Some of your leaders will seem like "naturals," but most will need help in some areas. It is worth the extra time to teach refined leadership skills in your students so that they can be small extensions of you.

The leadership camp is all about preparing your leaders for the rest of the band. You should rehearse them like a small version of the band. Give each member opportunities to lead the group. Allowing them to practice in this manner will allow them to get comfortable giving commands, providing direction, and staying on task.

For an example of a leadership camp schedule, see the sample itineraries.

Marching Band Leadership Camp Example

Day 1

CHECK-IN AND REGISTRATION

Date: _____

On-campus students: Report to preassigned dorms for move-in at 9:00 a.m.–12:00 p.m.

Off-campus students: Report at 12:00 p.m. for lunch

12:00 p.m.–12:15 p.m.	**Report to Band Room for Lunch Ticket**
12:15 p.m.–1:00 p.m.	**Lunch**
1:00 p.m.	Settle in Dorms (Pay dues at the cashier office before 12:00 p.m. and bring receipt to the meeting.)
3:00 p.m.–3:30 p.m.	Registration and Section Leader Meeting with Drum Majors Instrument Distribution Location: Home Band Room (No specific attire required)
5:00 p.m.	**Dinner** (Change clothes for rehearsal)
6:30 p.m.	Opening Meeting and Physical Training Location: Home Band Room (Practice attire: black and white)
7:30 p.m.	Sectionals (Basic Commands)
8:15 p.m.	Team Building and Leadership Training No. 1 "SWOT Analysis"

8:30 p.m.	Music Rehearsal / Auxiliary and Percussion Sectionals New Personnel Advisors: Planning Session
9:30 p.m.	Team Building No. 2
10:00 p.m.	Band Service Project No. 1 Review and Dismissal

Pack for Leadership Retreat

Packing List: Toiletries, pool wear, change of clothes, 2016 band shirts, towel, soap, bath cloth and other hygienic necessities, hat, snacks, required medications

Marching Band Leadership Camp Example

Day 2

Date: _____

3:00 a.m	Report to Home Band Room Load Bags and Equipment (See Packing List)
3:30 a.m.	**Depart School**
6:30 a.m.	Arrive at Camp Location Physical Training Calisthenics (Report to Home Band Room)
7:30 a.m.	Breakfast
9:00 a.m.	Field Rehearsal (Report to New Band Room) Teach (Without Instruments) Stretches/Vocal Commands Basic Commands and Fundamentals of Drill Attention, Parade Rest, Left Face, Right Face, About Face Arm Swing, Leg Lift, MT, 8 to 5, TTR, Guide Right (Sweep the Field)
11:00 a.m.	Freshen up and Prepare for Music Rehearsal Snack
12:00 p.m.	Depart for Lunch and Music Rehearsal
12:00 p.m.	**Lunch**
12:45 p.m.	Warm-Ups / Music Fundamentals Music Rehearsal (Traditional Repertoire) (Auxiliary Separate Session)
2:00 p.m.	Team Building No. 3: Band Leadership Training "Instructional Tips for Effective Sectionals"
3:00 p.m.	Music Rehearsal (Traditional Repertoire) New Personnel Advisors: Planning Session
4:00 p.m.	Load Buses

6:00 p.m.   **Dinner and Relaxation**

7:30 p.m.   Clean Up

8:00 p.m.   Depart for School

11:00 p.m.   Arrive at School

Marching Band Leadership Camp Example

Day 3

Date: _____

10:00 a.m.	Band Service Project No. 2
11:30 a.m.	Lunch
1:30 p.m.	Warm-Up
	Sight Read, Show Music, and Stand Music
3:00 p.m.	Sectionals
4:30 p.m.	Music Rehearsal Check Offs
5:15 p.m.	**Dinner**
6:45 p.m.	Basic Commands and Fundamentals of Drill
	Teach *Pinwheels*, *Slant*, *Folds*, Drop-Offs, *Pinwheels*, *Slant*, *Folds*, *Flank*, *Shifts*, *Line Maneuver*, *Rotations*, *Backward March*, *Corps* (Without Instruments)
7:45 p.m.	Review Leadership Concepts
8:30 p.m.	Band Service Project No. 3: Prep for Band Check-In

Leadership Camp Discussions and Activities

TEAM BUILDING ACTIVITIES

Ice Breaker (Leaders)
Two Truths and a Lie

Name Recognition (New Personnel)
Name Game (Tennis Ball)

Character Building (Leaders)
Headband Game

Nonverbal Communication (Full Band)
Nonverbal Birthday
Snake

History (New Personnel and Full Band)
NCCU and Sound Machine Trivia
Crossing the Plank

Conflict Resolution (Leaders)
Solve this Conflict

LEADERSHIP DEVELOPMENT TOPICS

Review Director's Strategic Plan

SWOT Analysis and Overview
(Strengths, Weaknesses, Opportunities, Threats)
Where did we make improvements?
What are the positive attributes of our band? What needs work?
What does a band member look like? What should they know?

How to Run a Sectional

SMART Objectives

SMART is an acronym that stands for *specific, measurable, attainable, realistic, and timely.*

Conflict Resolution Examples

The Elephant's in the Band
The Habitual Rule Breaker
The Nonpracticing Member
The Excuse Maker
The Prankster
The Nonchalant
The Mad Bandsman

Chapter 10

FULL BAND ARRIVAL: SCHEDULE AND PROCEDURES

When it is time for the remaining band members to report to camp, you should immediately put the section leaders to work. Day 1 of full band camp is really focused on communication and logistics. Even though you have already provided the itinerary in advance, have your leaders send out reminders to their section members. Provide a template of a message that you want to send, if necessary. At your initial meeting, always begin with introductions so that the new personnel will be able to identify their section leaders and so that the leaders will get the opportunity to apply the concepts taught in the leadership camp. Give the leaders constant critique so that they will stay on their toes and keep their section members on their toes as well. This is a constant cycle of teaching leaders to pass on information. Hold them accountable. Provide feedback. Then put them back to work. As you prepare for day 1 of band camp, your schedule should include the following:

1. Slideshow or Overview of the Program
2. Principles of Musicianship

3. Calisthenics and Fundamentals of Drill
4. Team-Building Exercises
5. Band Culture, Traditions, and Past Practices
6. Sectional Management Tips and Conflict Resolution
7. Daily Rules, Operations, and Procedures
8. Student and Director's Goals for the Year

For an example of a full band camp schedule, see the sample itineraries.

Full Marching Band Camp Day 1

CHECK-IN AND REGISTRATION

Date: _____

On-campus students: Report to preassigned
dorms for move-in at 9:00 a.m.–12:00 p.m.
Off-campus Students: Report at 12:00 p.m. for Lunch

7:30 a.m.	Leadership Breakfast with Drum Majors
11:30 a.m.	Lunch
1:00 p.m.	New Personnel Settle in Dorms (Pay Dues at Bursar, Change Clothes for Meeting)
3:00 p.m.–	Band Check-In
3:45 p.m.	Instrument Distribution Location: Band Room (_____ Bldg.)
4:00 p.m.	Opening Meeting Location: Band Room (Black Concert Attire; Bring Change of Clothes)
5:00 p.m.	**Dinner**
6:30 p.m	Physical Training (Practice Attire: Black Shorts and White T-shirt)
7:30 p.m.	Sectionals (Basic Commands) for New Personnel and Section Leaders Veteran Band Member Meeting Location: Home Band Room
8:15 p.m.	Full Band: Basic Commands and Fundamentals of Drill

9:15 p.m.	Music Rehearsal / Auxiliary and Percussion Sectionals
10:45 p.m.	Team Building and New Personnel Meeting No. 1
11:15 p.m.	Dismissal

Marching Band Camp

Day 2

Date: _____

6:30 a.m.	Physical Training Calisthenics (Report Band Room)
7:00 a.m.	Breakfast

8:30 a.m.	Field Rehearsal (Report to Band Room)
	Teach (Without Instruments)
	Stretches / Vocal Commands
	Basic Commands and Fundamentals of Drill
	  Attention, Parade Rest, Left Face, Right Face, About Face
	  Arm Swing, Leg Lift, MT, 8 to 5, TTR, Guide Right

9:45 a.m.–
11:00 a.m.
	Warm-Ups / Music Fundamentals
	  Winds (Class Room A)
	  Percussion and Auxiliary Sectionals (Outside Locations)

11:15 a.m.	**Lunch**
1:30 p.m.	New Personnel Meeting No. 2 (Class Room A)
2:10 p.m.– 3:15 p.m.	Sectional Rehearsals (Class Room B) `Auxiliary Dance Fundamentals (Dance Room) Auxiliary Flag Fundamentals (Gymnasium) Percussion Fundamentals Material (Band Room)
3:30 p.m.– 4:30 p.m.	Brass/Woodwind Separate Sectionals (Recital Hall)
4:45 p.m.	Full Music Rehearsal (Band Room)
5:15 p.m.	**Dinner**

7:30 p.m.	Review Basic Commands and Fundamentals (Field)
	Teach Marching and Playing, MT, 8 to 5, TTR, Guide Right,
8:00 p.m.	Full Band Music Rehearsal
9:30 p.m.	Snack
10:00 p.m.	**Sectionals Memorization and Final Music Rehearsal**

Marching Band Camp

Day 3

Date: _____

9:30 a.m.	Full Band Field Rehearsal (Band Room) Teach Pinwheels, Slant, Folds, Drop-Offs (Without Instruments) Review MT, 8 to 5, TTR, Guide Right,
10:15 a.m.	Warm-ups / Music Fundamentals (Classrooms)
10:45 a.m.	Brunch
11:45 a.m.– 12:15 p.m.	New Personnel Meeting No. 3 (Class Room A)
12:30 p.m.– 1:30 p.m.	Sectional Rehearsals: Show Music (Class Room B) Auxiliary Dance Performance Material (Dance Room) Auxiliary Flag Performance Material (Gymnasium) Percussion Fundamentals (Band Room)
1:45 p.m.	Brass/Woodwind Separate Sectionals (Band Room)
3:30 p.m.	Break
4:00 p.m.	Full Band Rehearsal
5:15 p.m.	**Dinner**
7:30 p.m.	Section Leaders Drill Memorization (TBA Locations) Field Rehearsal (Report to Band Room) Review Basic Commands and Fundamentals of Drill Drill Stations Exercise: 8 to 5, TTR, Guide Right (Sweep the Field) Pinwheels, Slant,

Folds, Drop-Offs, Flank, Shifts, Line
Maneuver, Rotations, Backward March,
Corps. Flank, Shifts, Line Maneuver,
Rotations, Backward March, Rotations,
Marching and Playing

9:00 p.m.   **Break**
New Personnel Meeting No. 4: Give
Homework

9:30 p.m.   **Sectionals Memorization and Final Music
Rehearsal
Check-Up (Check-Off Tomorrow)**

Marching Camp

Day 4

Date: _____

10:30 a.m.	Brunch
3:00 p.m.	Sectionals
4:00 p.m.	Check-Offs
	Instrumentalists (Band Room)
	Auxiliary Sectionals (Gymnasium)
5:00 p.m.	Dinner
6:45 p.m.	Field Rehearsal (Report to Band Room)
	Review Drill Charts
	Teach Opening Sets 1–4
	Full Band Music Rehearsal (Show Music, Stand Rehearsal)
	Physical Training Calisthenics

Part C

SOUND LIVING

Chapter 1

CONCLUSION: LET THEM HATE

Here are the main lessons that I learned during my journey to "sound living."

1. *Haters have one job. That job is to hate.* Smile through all the public ridicule. Stay focused and don't deter from your plans. Every one who wants your job will always feel that they can do a better job, but so what? What other people think about you really isn't your business anyway. So don't get caught up with responding to negative comments about your program. Just keep working. Establish a vision for your group and work toward it on a daily basis. You will eventually get to a place where the fruits of your hard labor will be evident. It may be a slow process, and that is just fine. You can cook chicken in the microwave, but it is probably not a good method to use. Dream big for your ensemble. Set long-term and short-term goals and then go to work. And smile a lot. Haters really can't stand that.

2. *Keep a clean operation.* To be very direct, my supervisors told me, "Don't mess with the money or the kids." Fiscal management and accountability is very important. Keep very

good records. Always maintain a very clear teacher-student relationship. Don't cross those lines. Students are not your friends. Reestablish some old-school principles. Never allow them to call you by your first name. This will reinforce the levels in the student-teacher relationship.

3. *Study your craft.* Go to conferences. Network with colleagues. Get a mentor. If you become the smartest person in the room, then it is time to find another place to hang out. Always put yourself in environments where the people around you are smarter. Ask questions and apply the "good" answers to your teaching. Take advantage of the expertise of your colleagues. If you're a woodwind player and the director across town is a brass player, set up exchange rehearsals or offer to conduct a sectional rehearsal. You can't lose with a healthy collaboration of great minds.

4. *Take care of yourself.* This job is stressful. Find and make time for yourself. You must remain physically, mentally, and spiritually healthy. Keep a healthy diet. This can be difficult because of our long schedule. But just like you prepare your lessons, you can prepare your meal. Take one day on the weekend and prepare meals for yourself. If you can't take a nap during the day, don't stay up late. Go home, go to bed, and wake up early to finish your tasks. You will need your energy to deal with the stress of students, parents, and administrators. Avoid self-medicating because of stress. It is very easy to turn to alcohol or other toxins as a means of distressing or calming down at the end of the day. Given the nature of our jobs, stress reoccurs daily. This means that your self-medication will become a habit and habits become dependencies. You can replace this habit with daily exercise. Thirty minutes per day of exercise can do a lot for you physically. Mental and spiritual health can be achieved by finding a hobby, such as reading, playing games, performing on your instrument, attending church, or joining a nonmusical organization. It is very easy to lose yourself in the job. Don't

let the job define you. Stay active in the community. Develop a social life outside of your school. Get involved with your family and friends. Schedule the aspects that enrich you mentally, physically, and spiritually, just like you schedule your band performances. You are more important than your job. Your band doesn't belong to you. It belongs to the ones who come after you. It is simply your job to take care of it so that the future directors and students will be able to enjoy it. Do your part to leave it better than you find it and then give it back when your time is up. I've attended four funerals of band directors who died either on the job or while performing their jobs under very stressful situations. Don't let this job take you out.

5. *Work hard and then "quit" hard.* I quit every year. After fifteen years, I've learned that quitting is necessary sometimes. One of my students posted on his timeline, "Quitting is an option." He was right. Quitting, to me, is totally shutting off my job. Now I wake up early just to talk to my kids in the morning before school. I actually cut the grass, wash the cars, and take my wife to lunch in the middle of the day. I take time for naps. I read. I write. I take time to post stupid things on social media just to watch stupid people respond. I go visit family and friends. I meditate, and I listen to the silence. In that silence, I found my dreams again. I began to hear new things in my dreams. I found new aspirations. I heard new music, new sounds. I began to live again . . . I began to live soundly. I finally found "sound living."

Chapter 2

FORMS AND CHECKLIST: TEMPLATES FOR SUCCESS

Forms

December to May
1. Recruitment Packet
2. Director Contacts
3. Staff Contracts
4. Audition Sheets
5. Database

May
1. Scholarship Letter Recommendation
2. Scholarship Contract
3. Scholarship Dispersals

June
1. Preliminary Report
2. Band Camp Mailing (Determine Dues and Camp Date Approval)
3. Vendor List
4. Phone Contacts

5. Personnel Requisition (Staffing)
6. Season Schedule
7. Budget for Year

July
1. Scholarship Form
2. Recruitment Assessment (Admission/Financial Aid/Housing Deposit)
3. Health/Physical Form
4. Liability Form
5. Band Camp Registration
6. Band Camp Itinerary
7. Instrument Checkout
8. Band Handbook
9. Travel Agreement
10. Progress Report
11. Copy of Schedule Form
12. Conflict Form
13. Requisitions for Orders

August
1. Requisitions for Travel
2. Expense Reports
3. Band Class Syllabus

Other Forms
1. Proposals
   Scholarship Proposal
   Budget Increase Proposal
   Fundraising Campaign

2. Three-Year Vision

Summer Checklist

1. Camp Dates Approved
2. Inventory Complete
3. Instruments Repaired
4. Summer Mailing Complete
5. Music Arranging and Show Plan Done

Band Camp

1. Housing List Submitted
2. Cafeteria Services Requisitioned
3. Band Camp Supplies Purchased and Requisitioned
4. Section Leaders Called
5. Music (Basic Repertoire) Organized
6. Music Emailed
7. Camp Forms Ready
8. Field Reserved
9. Camp Itinerary Emailed to Campus Security
10. Asthma Patients and Other Illnesses or Allergies Identified
11. Uniform Fitting Done
12. Summer Uniform Orders Ready
13. Auxiliary Uniform Orders Ready
14. Class Syllabus Complete
15. Transportation Request Done for Fall
16. Music for Fall Convocation Chosen
17. Student Committees Set

Acknowledgments

Special thanks goes out to my lovely wife and kids who had to share me with the band world for the last fifteen-plus years.

Shout out to my immediate family—Mom, Papa John, Garlinda, Jay, and Mac. Thanks for loving, protecting, teaching, and disciplining me as the youngest child and baby brother. I love y'all.

Big shout out to all my extended family for your support throughout the years.

Thanks to all my music teachers and influencers, beginning with Ms. Brown, my uncles, band directors, instructors, and my fraternity brothers and sorority sisters.

A huge shout out to all the colleagues whom I've worked with or supervised over the years. You taught me about the power of professional collaborations and teamwork.

I will forever be grateful for my experiences at all the colleges that I've attended, but I want to take the opportunity to pay homage to the historically black colleges and universities that shaped my life. My experiences there prepared me for any situation.

Finally, thanks to all my students whom I have taught, coached, mentored, parented, housed, fed, befriended (as adults, of course), disciplined, kicked out, scolded, and loved. Without you, there is no me. This book may not be totally for you, but it is about you. Thank you for providing me with a story to share to the world.

CPSIA information can be obtained
at www.ICGtesting.com
Printed in the USA
BVHW03*1011200718
522187BV00005B/34/P